THE
SOUL JOURNEY

HOW SHAMANISM, SANTERÍA, WICCA, AND CHARISMA ARE CONNECTED

EVP

by Kent and Katie Philpott

The Soul Journey:
How Shamanism, Santería, Wicca, and Charisma
are Connected

All rights reserved
Copyright © 2014 by Kent A. Philpott

Published 2014 by
Earthen Vessel Publishing
San Rafael, CA 94903
www.evpbooks.com

Interior Book Design and Layout by
Katie L. C. Philpott
Cover Image by Carl Laur

ISBN: 978-0-9703296-1-5 (print version)
Library of Congress Control Number: 2014909241

ISBN: 978-0-9898041-0-3 (ebook version)

ACKNOWLEDGMENTS

N early three years in process means that a group of people have been directly involved in seeing the book come together:

Thanks to Chuck Munson, Michelle Shelfer, and Stephanie Adams for their eagle proof-reading eyes. Thanks to Christina Milner-Rose for classroom feedback and the Foreword. Thanks to Richard Haskell for first bringing the subject of Santería to our attention, which then led to further connections.

Thanks to Roxana Aviles of El Salvador for working on the Spanish version so it reads properly, and due to the multi-cultured nature of the various religious groups involved, this is not a simple project. The same is true for Heirie Murakami for her preparation of the Portuguese language work and for contributing her experience and knowledge of Santería as experienced in Brazil as Candomblé. Likewise, Sika Amados for a French translation using knowledge of animistic African religious influence in her native country of Togo in West Africa.

Carl Laur created the cover image.
Contact him: life@carlwlaur.com

CONTENTS

FOREWORD

As an anthropology professor teaching comparative religion, I would list this book as a recommended text, as Kent Philpott has been a guest lecturer in my classes. His perspective is comparative like an anthropologist, yet, despite his evangelical Christian mission, he rejects certain views and behaviors of his more demonstrative and trendy Christian brethren.

In the Philpotts' comparative study of sects noted for high energy ecstatic states, they present the connection of monotheistic world religions with shamanism, a primitive and polytheistic category. The Philpotts argue that the pursuit of altered states of consciousness and trance in any religious category invites demonic possession. While the removal of demons is something Jesus and his disciples did regularly in healing the sick, shamanism claims to do the same. The Philpotts' book carefully delineates the difference between what Jesus did and what shamans do, and they urge charismatic sects within Christianity to stop using the shamanistic techniques of trance and altered states to attract adherents.

The focus here is on the deception that any highly agitated nervous system can cause in the consciousness of a human being, whatever their allegiance, including Christian. The Philpotts' targeted "altered states of consciousness" is a topic with a long history in religious studies. Lighting, music, repetitive rhythms and chants, drugs, incense, vestments, dance, pain or discomfort, stress through fasting or sleep deprivation, isolation or immersion in crowds, arduous pilgrimages, etc., have all been devices to facilitate religious experience in the participant. These devices and other rituals, including the apparent healing of the body or mind, getting "out of the body" and into transcendence, and communing with the spirits or gods, have experiential power to persuade seekers of the truth of the religion.

Kent Philpott is a Christian minister for whom the truth of religion is important. His evangelical mission is necessarily exclusive, not inclusive, meaning he doesn't believe that all paths lead to the same God. Even within Christianity he opposes some sects as potentially harmful to the Christian gospel message and to the practitioner. While that is the thesis of the book, descriptive accounts of each of the religions are analyzed from a unique perspective.

Aware of the inroads that primitive and new pseudo-primitive religions like Wicca have made into the urban landscape, Philpott opposes them as deceptive in their practices and claims. The "new" old religions, like Santería, sanitized of sacrificing chickens or other animals, can appeal to a contemporary society weary of technology and looking to put their money and devotion into something more earthy, participatory, mysterious, and ancient. He warns against the rising popularity and addictive aspects of these polytheistic belief systems and also against the new revealed truths and practices of established monotheistic Christianity because of the similarities he points out.

Specifically, Philpott warns all to avoid undercover shamanism invading modern culture and even Christianity, and for a specific reason. He demonstrates how the doorway to demonic invasion is unlocked via the trance states found in such religious activities. The features they have in common are cogently presented and clear. He more generally warns against psychological entrapment by techniques that have a long history of co-opting wishful thinking and resulting in enslavement to a cult.

The youth in my classes would do well to read it and be armed.

Christina Milner-Rose Ph.D.

PREFACE

I t all began with a study of Santería, which had been prompted by an inquiry from a woman who wanted help in discouraging her son from going to Cuba for initiation into that religion. Neither of us had ever heard of Santería, but saw very quickly that it was a religion built around magic, fortune telling, and mediums. After further research, we realized it was based on something far more primitive: animism and the system of spiritualistic religion commonly referred to as shamanism.

Santería is a major world religion that likely originated in West Africa among the Yoruba tribe.[1] It initially took root in Latin America via the sixteenth century slave trade and has been making its appearance in North America during the last century. Our study of Santería also led us to Wicca (loosely known as the religion of witches), of which we had been only minimally aware. Internet searches for details on Santería and Wicca stunned us. In one book after the other we slowly unwrapped the central aspects of these growing religious world views.

One might think that these religions were very different from one another; however, the connections were obvious. More than one writer identified the connecting 'dots': what they have in common is the *trance state* or *altered state of consciousness*.

After we finished researching the material on Santería and

---

1   In the last two years since Kent's YouTube videos on Santería were published, a number of respondents stated the origin was something other. However, most scholars agree that the worship of the orishas came out of West Africa, since the slave traders brought so many West Africans to the New World. It is likely that orisha worship evolved over many centuries and among many different tribes and people groups.

Wicca, we interviewed a Zen Buddhist master acquaintance about trance states. This expert in Zen told us about the Buddhist form of meditation he called "concentration." And he admitted it involved entering into a state other than the normal human consciousness. At the conclusion of our discussion he recommended that we read the author Mircea Eliade, an ethnologist whose book on shamanism opened up yet a further new world. After plodding through two of Eliade's works, *From Primitives to Zen* and *Shamanism*, it became clear that something even more basic lay behind Santería and Wicca, and that was shamanism. Our new search yielded a long list of books, and one by one they began to arrive in the mailbox. Now that the dots were connecting, it became imperative to write about our findings.

A further shock came when we noticed the word "charisma" in books on shamanism and Wicca in particular. It was clear what was meant: charisma involves states of mind, though rooted in and oriented toward Christianity, that resemble certain aspects of the aforementioned religious expressions.[2]

Thus, what started as a little booklet grew into something resembling an actual book, but it had to be so, since the trail of connecting dots had lengthened significantly.

This book is the result of that research. Our purpose is

---

2   Most English dictionaries define *charisma* as a trait of personal magnetism that draws people to follow those who have it. Occasionally an entry exists for *charismatic*, and generally describes Christian religious groups who stress the importance of the "charismatic gifts" as mentioned in the New Testament. We use the term charisma, not capitalized, to refer to kinds of worship wherein light, medium, and even deep states of trance are experienced, whether intentionally or unintentionally sought for. Usually such worship is characterized by mind numbing music, oft-repeated praise formulas, and non-choreographed dancing with eyes closed, and this for long periods. The goal of the worshipper is to connect with the Holy Spirit and be open to receive power, knowledge, and miracles. For some, mindfulness and thinking are considered impediments to being "filled with the Spirit." We are not referring to any particular denomination or church.

to inform others about shamanism, Santería, and Wicca in a manner not usually considered, which is to reveal and expose their underlying connections. Then, we want to caution fellow Christians that certain popular worship experiences are able to move worshippers into altered states of consciousness and are therefore potentially dangerous.

There is a larger reason for writing this book than simply providing information about spiritual and religious practices that are growing in popularity, especially among the youth of the world. Certainly we are all free to choose what we will do with our lives, but it is not always completely clear what is involved in some of our choices and what the consequences might be. In our view, the major issue associated with the trance state is that the spirits, helpers, guides, ancestors, elves, animal familiars, gods, goddesses, and so on, are not at all benign and harmless; radically to the contrary, they are actually unclean demonic spirits.

Many will vehemently disagree with us and already do so, as evidenced by comments and emails received in response to Kent's videos created on YouTube, articles Katie has posted at www.earthenvesseljournal.com, and various essays on the subject that have appeared in different places.

What proof do we offer for our conclusions? This is a fair and right question to ask, considering how many people's spiritual and religious practices are the foci of this book. Our answer is based on biblical material, on personal experience going back to work in the Haight-Ashbury District of San Francisco with the counterculture beginning in 1967, on testimony from those who have had demons cast out of them (which entities had gained entrée through the practices under consideration), and most significantly, on the written accounts of proponents of these religious practices.

Some people who are involved in Santería, Wicca, and shamanism have come to realize they have really been interacting with evil spirits, but they have decided to continue their involvement and have not adopted a Christian worldview. In addition, many of these practitioners do not realize that the beings and spirits they have been encountering are real entities and not merely part of their own thought processes. When it becomes clear that they are actual entities, the question must be, What are they?

The subject of this book is not a trivial pursuit; it is the difference between truth and error, life and death, and even eternal life and eternal death. Our plea is for the reader to examine the material and not judge prematurely. Let the truth be the truth and let the desire for the truth overcome fear and the risk of embarrassment.

As an editorial note, starting with the Introduction and continuing through the remainder of the book, all material written in the first person singular refers to Kent Philpott, while other significant research, writing, and editing is by the hand of Katie Philpott.

INTRODUCTION

S hamanism, Santería, Wicca, charisma, Christian mystics, the "trance state," and even the "soul" are connected. This book explores how that is so.

There are two sections to the book. One is composed of essays that were originally written for Earthen Vessel Publishing's online journal.[1] After the decision was made to bring them together in a book, a second section was added to include topics that relate to the first section.

Shamanism is the subject of the first essay, but it wasn't even on my radar until it was apparent that Santeria and Wicca 'sit' on top of shamanism, the underlying system.

Santería was the initial target of my work, and I could not help but entitle that essay "From Slavery to Slavery," since slave traders brought the Yoruba or West African worship of the *orishas* to the New World. In my view, the enslaved Africans therefore had two masters, one human and the other spiritual.

Wicca is a form of neo-paganism that is most familiar in contemporary American culture, and my research clearly revealed that it is thoroughly connected with shamanism.

Charisma would not have been included if it were not for my finding its reference in books on Santería and Wicca, used in a way that I first considered disingenuous. The word *charisma* is connected to a Christian term, *charismatic*, and is associated with the exuberant, even wild forms of worship found mainly among Pentecostals.[2] For many years I considered myself charismatic, and in many ways I still do. However, the kind of charisma with which the proponents of Santeria

---

1   www.earthenvesseljournal.com

2   See definition of *charisma* and *charismatic* in the Preface.

and Wicca identify involves altered states of consciousness. They are, in effect, saying, "See, the Christians are doing it, too."

Contemplative Prayer is another term found among Christians, and I am quite familiar with it. "Contemplative Prayer" is the title of a seminar that was part of a theological doctrinal program I completed in 1980. Upon re-examination of this practice, it has become evident that some aspects of contemplative prayer, or "deep meditation," depend upon the trance or altered state of consciousness. After considerable inner debate, I feel justified in connecting the trance dots all the way to this rather popular form of prayer and meditation.

In the last of the essays of section one, I attempt to make my case for a definite connection between each of the above.

The need for a second section, albeit a much shorter one, became clear. It was necessary to consider Yoga, Zen, meditation in general, plus a significant concept common to nearly every world religion and without which there is no shamanism, Santería, or Wicca. That is the concept of "soul." Here I run counter to a majority of Christians, but there is a reformation underway in understanding that this concept of soul is actually a Greek and not a Christian philosophical construct. More Christians are talking about the difference than ever before.

There is a "Biblical Matters" essay that was necessary, because readers of the first section objected by pointing to trance states presented in the Bible. Not everyone will be satisfied with my response.

Several contemporary examples of movements that come under the general category of charisma are included.

And lastly, there is the "Bottom Line."

SECTION ONE

This section consists of the major chapters of the book: Shamanism, Santería, Wicca, Charisma, Christian Mysticism, and Biblical Matters. Most of these began as stand-alone essays, and some were published in Earthen Vessel Publishing's online journal:
www.earthenvesseljournal.com.

CHAPTER ONE

SHAMANISM: THE BASELINE

S hamanism "is a methodology, not a religion" according to Michael Harner.[1] If not a religion, it is a spiritual system and worldview that underlies religious systems. Since the 1970s, shamanism has enjoyed a resurgence or revival, especially in the United States and Europe. According to Michael Harner and others, five things are responsible for this revival: (1), the use of LSD and other mind expanding hallucinogens, e.g., ayahuasca;[2] (2), soul survival following near-death experiences; (3), use of monotonous percussion sound to enter altered states of consciousness; (4), a multitude of practices under the general rubric of holistic health; and (5), the acceptance in traditionally Christian cultures of a wider range of spiritualities, some flowing from the East and others springing from the revival of paganism, centered on the belief that the planet is alive and spiritual in its essence.

Following now is an explanation of the core aspects of shamanism, including general origins, how it works, and what it influences.

---

1   Michael Harner, *The Way of the Shaman*, HarperOne, 1980, 1990, xiv.

2   Harner states, pages xv and xxv, that one may "will" one's way into a SSC or shamanic state of consciousness, thus escaping the rigors involved to do so for the traditional shaman, which typically necessitate years of meditation, prayer, or chanting.

ANIMISM – THE FOUNDATION FOR SHAMANISM

Animism is the ism that forms the foundation for all forms of shamanism. Animism encompasses the belief that there is no separation between the spiritual and physical world, and that souls or spirits exist not only in humans but also in animals, plants, and all living things as well as rocks, mountains, rivers, and other geographical features. Examples of animism can be found in forms of Shintoism, Hinduism, Buddhism, Jainism, ancient forms of paganism, Islam, and Neo-Pagan practices such as Wicca.[3]

In the animistic worldview, spirit, soul, or mind is in all, whether organic or inorganic, and soul is in people but has an existence apart from the body.[4] The spirit or soul can be communicated with and manipulated to some degree. Spirit may be understood as energy, force, or that which is part of the "Supreme," the "One," the "All."

THE SHAMAN

The origin and definition of the word "shaman"[5] is variously and ambiguously described; more important is what the shaman does. Siberian origins of the word have been proposed, either from the Siberian tribes Tungas or the Evenki. Ethnologists and anthropologists have grouped witches, witch doctors, medicine men, seers, wizards, sorcerers, magic men, and holy men with shamanism, with shaman becoming the catchall term for these individuals.

Spirit and soul are closely related terms and are concepts that are essential to shamanism. Most shamans hold that human beings have more than one soul, the more the better.

---

3 Discussed in detail in chapter 3.

4 Animism is not pantheism, which means all is God. It is not panentheism, which means that God is in everything. Animism sees all things as having mind, soul, or spirit and are thus alive and can be communicated with, appealed to, placated, and prayed to.

5 In the word shaman the "a" is short as in *shahmahn*.

The shaman is able to work with spirits and has the power to usher a soul to heaven or retrieve a soul from hell. He is a mediator of and traveler between the visible and invisible worlds.

Anthropologist David Stern says shamans "believe that unseen spirits permeate the world around us, act upon us, govern our fates. By turn doctors, priests, mystics, psychologists, village elders, oracles, and poets, they are the designated negotiators with this hidden reality, and they occupy an exalted position within their societies."[6] Stern further says there are many different forms of "shamanisms" but the common thread is "the ecstatic trance, or soul journey, as it's sometimes called, a signature phenomenon."[7] By means of ecstasy, meaning a trance state or altered state of consciousness, the shaman connects with spiritual powers for healing and other services beneficial to the community he or she serves. Harner puts it this way: "A shaman is a man or woman who enters an altered state of consciousness – at will – to contact and utilize an ordinarily hidden reality in order to acquire knowledge, power, and to help other persons."[8]

The shaman is the priest from primitive eras who has survived into the modern age.[9] Shamanism may well be the most practiced religious or spiritual form in the world. Shamans are everywhere and operate in the world's largest religions. But there is no individual known as a shaman in Islam, Buddhism, Hinduism, Sufism, Sikhism, Taoism, Shinto, Christianity, and others. Nevertheless, shamanism is present in each of these, though often in disguise.

---

6   David Stern, "Masters of Ecstasy" *National Geographic*, December 2012,   http://ngm.nationoalgeographic.com/2012/12/shamans/stern-text.

7   Ibid.

8   Harner, *The Way of the Shaman*, 25.

9   It is possible that rudimentary forms of shamanism existed 40,000 years ago.

Shamanism is intimately intertwined with modern paganism such as Wicca; in fact, Wicca may be classified as a form of shamanism. A book on Wicca could just as easily be described as a book on shamanism, and vice versa.

Shamanism touches Christianity by connection with Santería,[10] though Santería is not classified as part of Christianity. Santería, loosely translated as "that saint thing," blended to a certain degree with Roman Catholicism. Its shamanistic male and female priests, called santeros, santeras, and babalawos, are often mistaken as Christian.[11]

Charisma[12] does not directly connect with shamanism but does so indirectly by means of the trance state.

ORIGINS OF SHAMANISM

Mircea Eliade, the French anthropologist whose book, Shamanism, is regarded as the classic work on the subject,[13] concludes that shamanism developed in Siberia and central Asia somewhere in the Paleolithic era and is thus tens of thousands of years old. Harner agrees that shamanism is at least twenty to thirty thousand years old.[14] Eliade proposes that it spread when the shamans from Siberia migrated into all of Asia, Indo-Europe, and Africa, and also crossed over the frozen bridge between present day Russia and Alaska, with shamanistic views and practices continuing southward down to the tip of Argentina. It has flourished ever since.

Others suggest it developed independently in various locales due to the tendency of humans to inadvertently expe-

---

10 See chapter 2

11 Crystal Blanton, a Wiccan high priestess, combines the worship of the Santerían goddess Yemaya with her witchcraft. See *Sage Woman* issue 84, pp. 27-30.

12 See chapter 4.

13 Mircea Eliade, *Shamanism: Archaic Techniques of Ecstasy.* trans. Willard R. Trask. Princeton: Princeton University Press, 2004.

14 Harner, *The Way of the Shaman,* 51.

rience trance states. Roger Walsh, Ph.D., M.D., author of my favorite book on the subject of shamanism, poses the possibility that human experiences "such as isolation, fatigue, hunger, or rhythmic sound" might lead to the discovery of altered states of consciousness, chief among them being the trance state.[15] Since such experiences are common to humankind, trance states would be a shared phenomenon and form a context for spiritual development in many places.

Michael Harner suggests that the altered state of consciousness is an evolutionary adaptation that helps secure the survival of the species. He views the SSC or "shamanic state of consciousness" to be superior to the OSC or "ordinary state of consciousness."[16] Indeed, athletes, artists, musicians, writers, and even scientists have explored the SSC as a means of developing their particular skills and insights. The basic fact that shamanism around the globe shows an obvious uniformity, Harner says, points to a possible DNA encoding mechanism that eventually yields something akin to shamanistic views and practices. Shamanism is worldwide, Harner insists, because "it works."[17]

Perhaps each of the above views has some validity and may even have worked in combination. The seemingly universal quest for altered states of consciousness may be the central factor for the similarity of expressions in shamanism wherever they are found. It is in the trance or passive state that, in my view, a human is most open to contact with spirits, regardless of what they are called. One objective of this book is to focus on the identity and nature of the spiritual entities that make shamanism and its offshoots work. The issue of what these spirits are is much debated. Most observers and practitioners are aware that not all spirits are beneficial; few, however, see

15 Roger Walsh, *The World of Shamanism: New Views of an Ancient Tradition* (Woodbury, Minnesota: Llewellyn Publications, 2007), 18.

16 Harner, *The Way of the Shaman*, xxiv.

17 Ibid., 51.

them as evil or identified with the demonic.

THE SHAMAN AND ECSTASY

Shamans are identified with ecstasy. Not all those who engage in ecstasy or trance states are shamans, but the shaman's claim is that his or her[18] soul, while in the state of ecstasy or trance, leaves the body and ascends to the sky or descends to the underworld.

Anthropologist David Stern quotes a shaman named Dorzhiyev who lives in the Russian Republic of Buryatiya in Siberia and who described the shamanic trace experience:

> As you start to fall into the trance, you feel some force of energy coming closer to you. You can't see it – it's like a human form in the fog. And when it comes even closer, you see who it is, that it is a spirit. Someone who lived long ago. He enters you, your consciousness departs. Your consciousness goes to somewhere beautiful. And the spirit takes over your body.[19]

To obtain the shamanic vision, i.e., knowledge of and contact with the spirit world, the trance state is essential. The most experienced and respected shamans are able to enter into a trance easily and quickly. Some means of doing so are dancing, chanting, repetitive singing, deep meditation or contemplation, sensory deprivation, sensory overload, and hallucinogenic drugs like ayahuasca, peyote, mushrooms, LSD, tobacco smoke, alcohol, or any of the preceding in combination.

Shamans have contact, even relationships, with spirits. A spirit may identify itself as the soul of a dead person, a nature spirit, a mythical or real animal, or a god or goddess. There are many possibilities, and the spirits' purpose is to assist the sha-

---

18 Shamans may be male or female, especially in more recent times. From here on I will use either he or him in references to actual shamans.
19 David Stern, "Masters of Ecstasy"

man. The identity of the "spirit" is of vast importance to our study. Are shamans correct in their identification? Our thesis says no, and further explanation follows.

SHAMANS AND THEIR POWER

Shamans are said to control the spirits rather than be possessed by them. This is said to be the mark of the practiced and mature shaman, but at times and in certain places, shamans can be under the control of a spirit. If all proceeds as the shaman wants, however, and he is the controller, the spirit guide or helper will give him the ability to communicate with the dead, other spirits, souls, and demons.

Since the dead are said to know things about the unseen world that living humans cannot, the shaman also engages in divination or fortune telling. This form of shamanic work may be referred to as "journey foreseeing." As in SSC, the shaman journeys, usually with the help of a spirit animal or plant helper, to see what will be in store for a client. In addition, a "shaman may engage in clairvoyance, seeing what is going on elsewhere at the present moment."[20]

Shamans are healers and have learned secrets to work cures. During long periods of human history, the shaman with his knowledge of healing techniques and the application of various herbs was the only medical practitioner available.

In a tribe or society, Shamans are the elite due to their unique ability to manipulate the unseen world. The shamans are the mystics of any religion, those who are comfortable with the forces of the spirit. In a trance or ecstasy, the shaman is able to determine the cause of an illness and find the means for a cure. The shaman is the holy man who accompanies the dead to the "Realm of Shades" and serves as a mediator between them and their gods, celestial or infernal, greater or lesser. The shaman is the specialist in the human soul; he alone

---

20   Harner, *The Way of the Shaman*, 55.

'sees' it and can learn its destiny.

While shamans use power derived from spirits and souls of the dead to achieve certain ends such as healing of disease, the same power can be directed toward harmful or negative purposes. The shaman may be either a healer or a sorcerer, depending mostly on the needs and desires of a client. Shamans recognize the reality of demonic or evil spirits but are supposedly not alarmed or influenced by them. This is also said of the santeros, santeras, and babalawos of Santería and of the witches of Wicca. Each and all of these are aware of the "negative" forces, as they may call them, but they pride themselves in their high intentions and assert that they are careful not to use the power they have for harmful purposes.[21]

As will be shown, their assumption that there is a difference between good and bad spiritual entities is a superficial and false conception.

There is a "beautiful side of evil,"[22] which is initially alluring and attracts adherents to shamanistic systems, so it is not surprising that shamanistic techniques and practices are attracting new followers around the world. More alluring than beauty, however, is the quest for power. Beauty is the bait; power is the hook.

SOURCES OF SHAMANIC POWER

The list of the sources of shamanic power is akin to what the Wiccans utilize. Several books I consulted on shamanism, as previously mentioned, could just as easily have been about neo-paganism, particularly Wicca, and the reverse is also true. The concepts are virtually identical, and this is most evident

---

21 Based on emails I have received responding to essays I have written on Santería and Wicca there seems to be no hesitation to send beings from the nether regions to do me harm. These messages have arrived weekly for years now, and most are obscene.

22 A phrase coined by Johanna Michaelsen in her book of the same name, in which she describes her exit from involvement in the occult.

when speaking of the shaman's power sources. The sources are (1) power animals, (2) spiritual teachers or guides, (3) objects infused with power, such as a rattle, drum, totem, etc., and (4) the elements of nature such as quartz crystals, the four directions of north, south, east, and west or the basic elements of fire, water, earth, and air.

THE GUARDIAN SPIRIT AND OTHER HELPING SPIRITS

Each shaman will have at least one guardian or helping spirit which is usually represented as an animal, e.g., wolf, coyote, or eagle. This spirit may be with the shaman from birth but may leave after a period of time and need to be retrieved.

The guardian spirit may be referred to as a friend, companion, angel, or familiar.[23] The shaman uses these spirits while in an altered state of consciousness or SSC.

The shaman acquires spirits from three categories: animal helping spirits, spiritual teachers (dead or still living), and souls of the dead (often more than one). Spirit teachers can access power or directly provide power to the shaman, who may use rattles or drums to summon spirits and may appeal to the elements and the four directions of the planet, which the shaman believes are alive, to obtain power. Living spirit teachers or guides may be elders in the community. Non-living guides may be spirits of community ancestors, local deities, aliens from outer space, and mythical or legendary gods and goddesses, including those from the Greco/Roman pantheon. Shamans working in the Christian tradition claim angels as guides. The teachers and spiritual guides may appear in a human-like form, animal-like form, as a light or aura, or in a symbolic form.

Power animals such as eagles, coyotes, deer, horses, fish, or others can transport the shaman to the "other world." This is

---

23 Interestingly, in the King James Version of the Bible demonic spirits are sometimes called "familiars," e.g., Lev. 19:31; Deut. 8:11; 1 Sam. 28:7; Isa. 29:4.

done in a trance state, and the shaman often carries or wears something that symbolizes the animal, such as a feather or the image of a coyote painted on a garment. They access the power of the animal represented. Some shamans have a stick horse fetish they "ride" on their journeys.

The drum and rattle of the shaman may be referred to as a "horse," "mount," "steed," or "canoe" that serve to transport him to the "lower world" or "upper world." The beat of the drum and noise of the rattle, performed just right, are the means of powering the journey.[24] Harner states that research "has demonstrated that drumming produces changes in the central nervous system" and that "the shaking of the shaman's rattle provides stimulation to higher frequency pathways in the brain than does the drum, reinforcing the drum beats and further heightening the total sonic effect."[25]

Power objects are also important in the shaman's tool palette. Ceramic depictions of a turtle, bird, pine cone, egg, and other objects of nature are examples, and they need periodic feeding or re-energizing.[26] Shamans must placate and feed their power animals periodically in order to keep them from wandering off and to thus maintain empowerment.[27] There is a connection apparent here with the feeding of the Santerían "otanes," which will be described in the next chapter.

POWER SONG

Every shaman needs a power song. Michael Harner's own power song is as follows:

Stanza one:

---

24 Harner, *The Way of the Shaman*, 65.

25 Ibid., 66.

26 The same concept is found in Santería and is one of the reasons animals are routinely sacrificed, as the blood is said to feed the power objects, usually a representation of an orisha, which is a Santerían god or goddess.

27 Ibid., 125.

I have spirits,
Spirits have I.
I have spirits,
Spirits have I.
I have spirits,
Spirits have I.
I, I, I.
This is repeated three times then on to stanza two:
My spirits
Are like birds,
And the wings
And bodies are dreams.
I have spirits,
Spirits have I.
I, I, I.[28]

The second stanza is repeated three times then back to the first stanza; this pattern is continued for as long as needed to enter into to an altered state.

QUARTZ CRYSTALS

Quartz crystals are considered to be power objects. They are thought to have great spiritual significance, and thus shamans traditionally carry one or more on their person, preferably in a pouch made of a wild animal skin. The bag is the "bundle" or the medicine chest of the healing shaman. Many shamans enter into a special relationship with their crystals much like one would with a pet, even to the point of feeding them with substances like tobacco juice. Once again we see, or will see in the next chapter, a connection with certain Santerían practices.

POWER PLANTS

In addition to power animals and quartz crystals, a sha-

---

28 Ibid., 94.

man will depend upon the power of plants; they serve as spirit helpers. Plant power is not as strong as the animal or guardian spirit but is nonetheless essential for certain ceremonies. A shaman may have only one or two animal helpers but may have hundreds of plant spirit helpers. Shamans will acquire power plants while wandering in deserts, forests, and other places where exotic plants grow. Once such a plant is discovered, the shaman develops a relationship with that plant.

THE RECRUITMENT AND INITIATION OF THE SHAMAN

There are generally three ways in which a person becomes a shaman. First is by heredity, from father to son or grandfather to grandson. This is referred to as "the hereditary transmission of the shamanic profession." Second is a spontaneous vocation, a call, or an election. This may occur when a person is healed through the agency of a shaman and is "called" at the same time. Third is a personal desire and decision to become a shaman. Shamans with either hereditary title or those elected spontaneously are considered the most powerful. The least powerful and respected are those who pursue the position through self-entitlement.[29] In some religions, shamans (holy men or medicine men) are sought among those who are peculiar or exhibit signs of what more cultured societies would term mental or emotional illness. The unusual person, perhaps exhibiting epileptic seizures or schizophrenic behavior, is looked upon as having a gift from the gods or spirits. The mentally ill, however, often prove to be unsuccessful mystics. Shamans from this third class are likely to lack religious content in their communications. In general, neither epilepsy nor any other brain or mental malady is considered genuine possession. More often the shaman is a very gifted person in the tribe or clan, an honored and respected person.

---

29 It is becoming increasingly common for single individuals, apart from a community, to seek to become a shaman. It is even possible to receive initiation via the internet.

Often a candidate for shaman will simply undergo a change, becoming more meditative, seeking solitude, sleeping a great deal, seeming absent-minded, having prophetic dreams, and sometimes having seizures. In more advanced cultures this is the more likely process.

In whatever way a person is recruited into shamanism, he is not recognized as a shaman until he has received two kinds of teaching. One is instruction or initiation through the ecstatic experience, meaning the entering into trance or having dreams or visions. The ease with which a shaman is able to enter into ecstasy is a sign of his power and ability. The second kind of teaching involves initiations and messages from either living or dead shamans. The teachings consist of mastering the complicated techniques of shamanism, learning the names and functions of the spirits, absorbing the mythology and genealogy of the clan, learning a secret language, and discovering how secret spiritual knowledge is accessed.

The initiation by way of the ecstatic or trance experience and the didactic initiation through rigorous learning may take place over a long period of time, perhaps years. More recently, the process has been significantly shortened, mostly among westerners.

THE THREEFOLD PATH OF INITIATION

The threefold path of initiation for the shaman is suffering, death, and resurrection. The would-be shaman suffers an illness, emotional or physical – the suffering; he then retreats from the tribe – the death; and re-emerges whole again – the resurrection. This may take place in reality, an event that the entire tribe witnesses. Or it may take place in an ecstasy, which the candidate experiences and then reports. In ecstasy the would-be shaman may see himself being dismembered, perhaps by birds or spirits tearing away flesh, blood, and bone; this is the suffering. The suffering results in the physical body's destruction and death. The body is then reconstructed or remade, thus completing the cycle with resurrection. Herein is the suffering, death, and resurrection, all of which the candidate for shaman must experience. Initiations are different among different people, but the same pattern is generally observed.

Once the shaman candidate has experienced the suffering and death, the resurrection, to be complete necessitates both an ascent to the sky where he speaks with the gods or spirits and a descent to the underworld where he converses with spirits and the souls of dead shamans.[30] Because the soul journey occurs only during ecstasy, the initiate must later recount his experience and thus satisfy the community that he is now a complete shaman.

The candidate must be expert at ascent and descent, because these will be major parts of his work on behalf of people who have lost loved ones or are suffering from some sort of illness. To accompany a deceased's soul to the sky – heaven – is a shaman's valued work. Of equal importance is the shaman's ability to retrieve a soul from the underworld – hell. These are among the chief functions of the shaman.

THE FIRST SHAMAN

There are legends that speak of a "first shaman" whose pride led him to enter into competition with the supreme god. This first shaman's body was made of a mass of snakes. The god sent down fire to burn the first shaman, but a toad emerged from the flames, and from this creature came the demons. I refer to this legend, because it reminds me of the biblical account of creation and the temptation of Adam and Eve in the Garden of Eden by the serpent (see Genesis chapter three). Certainly there are pronounced, even unmistakable, similarities between the two stories. That perhaps one

---

30 Ethnologists and cultural anthropologists who observe shamans in their natural setting are not attesting to the validity or reality of the gods, spirits, and souls. This is largely an issue avoided.

is dependent on the other seems reasonable, but which comes first is unknown. In terms of origins my view is that the story of the first shaman is borrowed from the biblical account and is a natural distortion of the story of creation accounts found in the Bible.

Among certain tribes the eagle is considered to be the creator of the first shaman.[31] Because eagles ascend to the sky, it is usual during ecstasy for the shaman to transform himself into an eagle in his ascents or be escorted there on the wings of an eagle. The eagle and other birds predominate in shamanistic ceremonies. Costume and ritual objects often utilize representations of various kinds of birds, including feathers and other bird-like features. The eagle's ascent into heaven occurs in the mind of the shaman and may be acted out by the shaman as an actor might act out a scene on a stage. To a considerable extent, shamans are also story-telling entertainers.

REAL OR IMAGINARY, INTERNAL OR EXTERNAL?

The issue then becomes whether what is reported by the shaman is real or imaginary. Various authors writing on shamanism, Santería, or Wicca hesitate to say that what goes on in an ecstasy has a separate reality apart from the mind. Others are clear, however, that what happens is real contact with the spirit world, that the animal spirits, souls of the dead, and so on, are real, although all taking place within the head and mind of the shaman, santero, witch, or medium.

Our research confirms that the locus of the shamanic experience is internal; neither the shaman nor his 'soul' leaves his body and travels into a spirit world. The shaman may think he is on a soul journey, but the journey takes place within the shaman. There is, however, an actual spiritual event occurring; the shaman is not merely imagining things. The soul journey is rather a deception that the indwelling or possessing spirits

---

31   M. Eliade, *Shamanism*, 68.

are perpetrating or performing. The shaman may or may not realize the difference.

Research for this chapter reveals that there is a marked distinction between the classical shaman and the westernized contemporary shaman. The classical or tribal shaman is less likely to be concrete as to what is occurring in his ecstasy. The modern western shaman is more likely to claim actual contact with an otherworld inhabited by real spirits, although not all westernized shamans are open and plain about this.

TUTELARY AND HELPING ANIMAL SPIRITS

A tutelary spirit is one that protects and guards the shaman. The tutelary spirit is even said to choose the shaman. A tutelary may give the shaman other helping spirits as well. Sometimes the tutelary spirit is female, even being called a "celestial wife." There is a close relationship between mystical and carnal love in shamanism, and there is no doubt that sexuality plays an important part in the shamanic story. A shaman can have sexual relations with female spirits or, if the shaman is female, with male spirits. This is the age-old story of the incubus and the succubus, which are spirits imitating humans and having sexual contact with them. In occult-oriented writings, spirits that impersonate men and women are reported to have actual sexual relations with the humans they possess.[32]

Tutelary spirits are also known as guardians. It is the tutelary spirit that the shaman 'calls up' in the séances, because they evidently have more power than the helping spirits. The majority of these spirits have animal appearances, and a chief characteristic of a shaman is the ability to adopt one of these

---

32 The suggestion of sexual relations with spirits may sound strange, but in my years of casting out demons, while rare, it was not absent. By spirits I mean demons. And typically, what began as pleasurable turned into something far less. It was the change that would motivate a person to get rid of the unclean spirit.

forms.[33] However, even though the shaman has 'face-to-face' experiences with gods and spirits and sees them, talks with them, prays to them, and implores them, he is in control, if at all, of only a limited number of them. Any spiritual entity invoked during a shamanic séance is not ipso facto one of the shaman's guardian or helper spirits.

A certain amount of confusion or lack of clarity persists in the accounts of the various spirits encountered in shamanic ecstasies. There is nothing in the literature that could be considered standardized or identified as authorized fact.

THE USE OF NARCOTICS IN ACHIEVING ECSTASY

By ecstasy is meant trance. Ecstasy is the moving out of a normal state of consciousness into a trance-like or altered state of consciousness. The trance entered into may be light, moderate, or deep. The experienced shaman can enter the deep trance easily. Other shamans, however, need help and resort to narcotics. Rum, tobacco juice, hemp smoke (cannabis), peyote, ayahuasca,[34] and psilocybin mushrooms, among others, may be used. Some shamans use a steam room or sweat lodge instead of a narcotic; combinations of the foregoing are often employed.

THE SHAMAN AS PSYCHOPOMP

A psychopomp is one who conducts souls to heaven or retrieves them from the underworld.[35] In Greco/Roman

---

33 It is not that the shaman suddenly looks like an animal but that he speaks like an animal and moves like an animal. This "act" is highly polished and miraculous in many ways, and it may continue for extraordinarily long periods of time, demanding strength and energy far beyond that of a normal human being.

34 This powerful hallucinogenic drug, also known as yage or yaje, can be highly toxic and dangerous.

35 From the ancient Proto-Germanic shamanistic world the word "hel" is used for the underworld and is where we get our English word "hell."

mythology, Hermes was a psychopomp.

Illness and disease in shamanistic societies are seen as possibly caused by a "rape of the soul" or the result of a soul wandering away or getting lost. The remedy is for the shaman to retrieve that soul, and if it is in either heaven or hell, the shaman has the power to go there, capture the soul, and induce it to come back into the patient's body.

In some cultures, soul retrieval is a major industry, because it is believed a person can have a number of souls. Only the shaman can work the cure; only he sees the spirits and knows how to deal with them. If the soul has left the body, only he knows how to overtake it, all of which is done in a trance.

Since sickness may be interpreted as a flight of the soul, the cure involves calling it back. If the soul has gotten lost or is merely wandering about, the shaman may read a litany of pleadings in which the patient's soul is implored to return from the distant mountain, valley, river, forest, fields, or from wherever it may be wandering.

SHAMANISTIC COSMOLOGY, THE THREE COSMIC ZONES, AND THE WORLD TREE

The shamanistic worldview sees the universe as having three levels – sky, earth, and underworld – that are connected by a central axis, hole, or axle, often referred to as the axis mundi. It is through this axis or hole that the three levels can be traversed. The gods descend from heaven through the hole and the souls of the dead descend through the hole to the subterranean regions. It is through this hole that the shaman, and only the shaman, can fly up in ecstasy to the celestial or down to the infernal regions.

A "center" is where there is a possible breakthrough in the axis or plane and, therefore, here is where spiritual power breaks through. In some circles these "vortexes" are known as places of power. In Marin County where I live and work is Mt. Tamalpais, and many neo-pagans consider that mountain to be a spiritually powerful place.

Shamanistic people will erect poles or pillars to mark a sacred place, and this pillar, pole, stake, or totem is treated almost as a god, often with a small stone altar placed at its foot to place offerings. These may be the center pole of a yurt, igloo, tent, home, lodge house, and so on. The pole is the link between heaven and earth. The hole in a tent that allows smoke out, as depicted in images of North American Indian tepees, also serves as access to heaven or hell.[36] In a larger sense, the "pole" can be a mountain, tree, pillar, pyramid, stele, and so on.

The cosmic tree is essential to the shaman, and that tree represents the World Tree. He may plant a birch tree, as representative of the World Tree, somewhere close to his residence and may make his drum from its wood. In climbing the ritual birch tree he believes he can reach the summit of the cosmic tree, heaven, the ultimate celestial place. He may keep artistic representations of the tree inside his dwelling place and on his drum. The tree connects the three cosmic regions of heaven, earth, and the underworld – the leaves reach heaven, and the roots extend to the underworld, while the trunk is the middle or present world.

The World Tree symbolizes the universe in continual regeneration, the inexhaustible spring of cosmic life, or the reservoir of the sacred. It also represents the idea of ultimate reality and immortality. The World Tree somehow becomes the Tree of Life and Immortality.

We see a connection with the biblical Tree of Life and also the Tree of the Knowledge of Good and Evil as described in Genesis chapters one to three. While it seems probable that there was borrowing, we found no evidence establishing a common origin.

---

36 "Hell" is sometimes used by various sources in place of "under-world" and other similar terms. Obviously some sort of borrowing was going on.

JOURNEYING IS A CORE SHAMANISTIC PRACTICE

Shamanism and Wicca clearly intersect and have a great deal in common when it comes to the concept of journeying. In shamanism, as discussed above, the journey is to the lower, upper, or middle worlds, and the destinations are keyed to the structure of the universe based on the World Tree. Again, the leaves represent the upper world, the trunk down to the ground is the middle world, and the roots are the lower world.

The journey begins only when the shaman is in the trance state, and any number of techniques can be used to enter the altered state of consciousness – dancing, drumming, chanting, meditating, taking hallucinogenic drugs, or breathing in specially prescribed techniques, and these, again, are often accompanied by infusions of tobacco, rum, and so on. These techniques are meant to trigger a shift to an altered or passive state of mind.

A power animal, such as an eagle, may be the form of transportation, and the reason for the journey usually has something to do with a healing or the solving of a problem for an individual or the community.

Once in one of the three worlds, a guide is necessary, perhaps the soul of a dead ancestor, and then the journey is underway. Shamans will see spirits or spiritual energies and will communicate with spiritual beings. Perhaps the shaman is on the hunt for a soul whose absence from the body of a patient has caused an illness.

The question always is: What is going on here? Is the shaman really encountering actual spiritual beings and souls of the dead? Over the course of my research on this, I have found writers to be fuzzy on this point. Some, however, state unequivocally that it is all real but occurs in the mind of the shaman, santero, or witch, etc. Psychiatry puts great pressure on writers, since it is generally thought that some of the things that Wiccans and shamans say might suggest mental or emotional pathology.[37] Whenever I engage in email exchanges with those who routinely go on soul journeys they will hesitate, equivocate, even become angry when I ask about the nature of the journeys and the entities encountered along the way. Any suggestion that there might be demonic spirits involved always ends the 'conversation'.

SHAMANISM IN NORTH AND SOUTH AMERICA[38]

The shaman's chief function is healing. Of first importance is the discovery of the cause of an illness. Generally, two kinds of illness are considered: one, due to the introduction of a disease-causing object, and the other, as a result of "soul loss," discussed earlier. In the first, the treatment is to expel the foreign object mystically. The second is to find and return the patient's fugitive soul. In the latter, the shaman is absolutely necessary, for only he can see the soul and capture it. In the first, a séance is conducted whereby helping spirits are summoned who reveal the problem and give the means to effect a cure. The shaman speaks as a medium and describes the activity and pronouncements of the spirits that take place while he is in a trance state.

The flight of the patient's soul may be due to dreams that frighten the soul away. Or it may be due to the soul of a dead person fearing a lonely journey to the "Land of the Shades" who then captures a living person's soul to take with him for comfort and protection. Or, a person's soul may simply stray from his body of its own accord.[39]

---

37 Occasionally, I have been able to establish contact via email with an author whose book I am studying. Usually I receive favorable responses, but once I bring up the above issue, the communication stops abruptly.

38 Rather than survey shamanistic expressions globally, we will confine ourselves to the Americas, which should be adequately representative. Though there are differences from place to place, tribe to tribe, the overall schematic is consistent. There will be, of necessity, considerable overlap with previous descriptions of shamanism.

39 The language we employ does not mean that we agree with the

When spirits or the souls of the dead carry off a soul, the shaman is believed to leave his body and enter either heaven or the underworld. The shaman's ecstatic journey is generally indispensable, even if the illness is not due to the theft of the soul by demons or ghosts. The shamanic trance forms part of the cure; whatever interpretation the shaman puts on it, it is always by means of his ecstasy that he finds the exact cause of the illness and learns the best treatment. The trance sometimes ends in the shaman's possession by his familiar spirits. In most cases possession merely puts the shaman's own helping spirits at his disposal.[40]

In the thinking of the North and South American Indians, every person commands a guardian spirit acquired by the same techniques the shaman uses to obtain his own spirits. The difference between layman and shaman is quantitative; the shaman commands a greater number of tutelary or guardian spirits and a stronger magico-religious power. In this respect we could say that every Indian "shamanizes," even if he does not consciously wish to become a shaman.

Many are familiar with what is called the Ghost-Dance, which continues among North American tribes to this day. To prepare for the coming of the savior of the race, there are five or six days of continuous dancing. The dancing is intended to put the participants into a trance where the dead are seen and conversed with. The dances are ring dances around fires; there is singing but no drumming.

DO SHAMANS EMPLOY TRICKERY?

Shamans can be entertainers, dancers, and singers who

---

shamanistic worldview; rather we are describing how it is for the shaman. Research and discussion with shamans have shed no light on how a soul strays from a body and whether this is the same as out-of-body experiences documented elsewhere.

40 What has just been described is the work of the shaman as psychopomp.

put on the best show in town. They may act out a wide variety of parts and will most often cast themselves as the heroes of the story. They can at one time be a bird and at another time a wolf. They are narrators of lively battles between the spirits and themselves; they are usually, but not always, the winner. But, is it just theater?

Shamans will admit to trickery, but it is excused as being for a good purpose. If a shaman secretly places a dead and bloodied worm in his mouth, then proceeds sucking at the body of a patient to the point of pain, then suddenly pulls the worm from his mouth – is this deception? Is it perhaps the employment of positive thinking or the use of a placebo? Is the victory shout of the shaman an authentic healing mechanism, or is it trickery?

Shamans do perform as described above, producing some ostensibly beneficial though questionable results. But what about the journeys they take to the lower, middle, or upper worlds? Do they really escort the dead soul to the final resting place? Do animal spirits assist them and give them power? Is it all in the mind or does it have a separate reality?

ADDITIONAL SHAMANISTIC PRACTICES AND CONCEPTS

The Craft of the Smith, the worker of fire and metal, ranks immediately after the shaman's vocation in importance. Smiths and shamans work together in many cultures. Smiths are said to have power to heal and even to foretell the future. Smiths, it is thought, are constantly threatened by evil spirits. The smiths' tutelary gods and spirits do not merely help them in their work; they also defend them against the onslaught of evil spirits.

Like the smiths, the shamans are masters over fire. But the shaman's power is greater. The smiths work with fire in forging their tools, most often weapons such as swords and knives. Control and power over fire is central, and protection from fire reflects shamanistic power and prestige.

Magical Heat is associated with control over fire, and advanced shamans are not merely masters over fire but can also incarnate the spirit of fire to the point where, during séances, they emit flames from their mouths or noses. The idea of mystical heat is not an exclusive possession of shamanism; it belongs to magic in general.

Often the shamanic ecstasy is not attained until after the shaman is "heated." There is every reason to believe that the use of narcotics was originally encouraged by the quest for magical heat. Smoke from certain herbs and the combustion of certain plants has the quality of increasing power. The narcotized person grows hot; narcotic intoxication is "burning."

The Bridge allows the shaman to travel from earth to heaven. By crossing the bridge that connects the world of the living and the dead while in ecstasy, the shaman proves that he is spirit, is no longer a human being, and thus may be able to restore the communication between the two worlds.

A myth that supports this concept is that the shaman does in ecstasy today what could be done by all human beings at the dawn of time. All humans could go up to heaven and come down again without recourse to trance. The shamans' ecstasy re-establishes the primordial condition of all mankind. We see here a restoration of ancient customs. For the shaman in ecstasy, the bridge, tree, vine, or cord, which originally connected earth with heaven, does so once again, even if only for an instant.

The Ladder concept is another means to the sky; it is another "road of the dead." In addition to the ladder as a way to heaven, there are stairs that reach from earth to the sky. The sky can also be reached by fire or smoke, by climbing a tree or a mountain, or by ascending a rope, a vine, the rainbow, or even a sunbeam. All these symbolic images of the connection between heaven and earth are merely variants of the World Tree and the Axis Mundi.

The shaman is an elect or privileged being, but he is not alone in being able to fly up to heaven or to reach it by means of a tree, a ladder, or the like. Other persons can do so as well: sovereigns, heroes, and initiates. Shamans differ from the other privileged categories by the one technique they employ, which is ecstasy. The shamanic ecstasy can be regarded as a recovery of the human condition before "The Fall."

Once again is found a connection with the opening chapters of Genesis. Before the rebellion against God called the Fall, in which humans broke the single command to not eat of the fruit of a certain tree, humans were living in the presence of their Creator. All their needs were met, and they had peace with each other, comfort in their environment, and even daily communication with God. But then this paradise experience ended, and the disobedient creatures that had been made in the image of God were forced to leave.

IS IT ALL REAL?

As spoken of previously, the core issue is whether the journeys into the otherworld and the spirits, souls, guides, and more that fill the world of the shaman are real or imagined. Some in shamanism do not care, as long as it serves some beneficial purpose, and those who maintain this have in mind consciousness expansion and relief from mental and emotional troubles.

My experience and research indicate that what is encountered in trance states can be either real or imagined. That said, it is the realness of the beings encountered by the shaman that is of chief concern. My position is that the beings are real but that they are not what they present themselves to be, e.g., the souls of deceased people who have returned to benefit those still living; they are, in fact, unclean or evil spirits. Obviously, many shamanism, Wicca, Santería, contemplative prayer, and charisma advocates will resist this conclusion, and while some will accept this evaluation, they will continue their practices, failing to realize the real danger. Most controversial among my opinions is that the way of the shaman is the road to demonization, the possession by unclean or evil spirits. I cannot play the role of either the anthropologist who merely observes and reports or the psychiatrist who believes the spirit world is part of the human brain. The spiritual realm that shamanism enters is ultimately horrific.

My abiding or overarching interest in shamanism and associated phenomena is that there are those who desire to be free from the beings or entities that they encounter and with which they have involved themselves. Finding that Satan does not cast out Satan, they turn in other directions to find relief. The only relief is, in fact, Jesus Christ, who triumphed over the demonic forces through His death and resurrection and alone has the power and authority to cast them out.

THE SHAMANIC LURE

Shamanism today is enjoying a revival of interest. The lure is primarily power, as stated earlier, and secondarily knowledge. The shaman's supposed control of spirits is a strong attraction. In our materialistic and scientifically-oriented world, it is a heady and life-changing experience to suddenly come into personal contact with spiritual entities and the vast spiritual universe. Jesus and the biblical writers were very much aware of this reality and spoke of how deceptive and dangerous it is.[41]

The lure of power and knowledge is found in many religious teachings. It is also present in Santería, Wicca, and charisma. There is an additional enticing element identified by many writers discussing Shamanism, Santería, and Wicca, and that is sexual. Writers in these areas will speak of the possibility of having sexual relations with guide spirits or even animal spirits. Despite attempts to blunt the sheer force of what they

---

41 See Matthew 24:24 and 2 Corinthians 11:14-15.

are saying by intimating that the sexual relations are merely bonding techniques, descriptions of these sexual relations are clearly powerful lures. Such spiritual experiences can be life-changing and addicting, and may extend for years. I've learned from counseling those who have been snared in this way that this thrilling allurement has a shelf life, and after that the product turns wormy.

CONNECTING POINTS

Similarities exist among shamans around the world, both in ancient and contemporary times. Some of these are a belief in a celestial god, shamanic initiation, relations with the souls of ancestors or dead shamans, relations with familiar spirits (relations that sometimes reached the point of "possession"), the conception of illness as soul loss or the intrusion of a magical object into the body of a client, and the shaman's insensibility to fire. These seem to have a broad similarity around the world.

The notion of the "soul" is fundamental to shamanic ideology. Wherever one looks at shamanism around the world, in both ancient and modern practices, the concept of a soul is indispensable. This cannot be over-emphasized. The belief in soul is as integral to shamanism as is the trance state or ecstasy. The origins of the concept, even the doctrine, of the soul are impossible to pin down, but it is certain that the ancient Greeks held to a dualistic philosophy that infiltrated many other philosophies or worldviews. Theirs was characterized by a good god struggling with an evil god, a division between light and dark, and a dis-integration of the individual into mind, heart, soul, and spirit on the one hand and the body or the flesh on the other. The spirit was considered good, while the body and all material was considered evil. This dualistic concept was imported to northern India around the onset of the first millennium before the Common Era and radically impacted the ancient form of Hinduism known then. The result was belief in an immortal soul that did not die with the physical body but transmigrated to other living forms. Thus the doctrine of karma developed and with it the idea of reincarnation. This is straightforward history.

Christianity was also impacted by Greek dualism in the fourth and fifth centuries after Christ, due to a revival of Greek philosophy sometimes called neo-Platonism. Although there is no concept of an immortal soul in the Hebrew or Greek biblical Testaments, the concept nonetheless entered the Church of that day and is embraced by a large percentage of Christians still. It survived to impact many of the churches that emerged out of the sixteenth century Reformation. The power of the doctrine of humans having an immortal soul is so strong among Christians that one who claims it is not a Bible-based concept is often labeled "liberal." What I call "soul confusion" has opened the door to some of the concepts found in shamanism.[42]

THE FUTURE OF SHAMANISM

Traditional shamanism exists in many parts of the world and has not undergone significant alteration over the millennia. However, modern shamanism greatly changed when it encountered contemporary western cultures. The acceptance of alternative or contemporary healing techniques has pushed shamanism into the current discussions of treatments for any number of physical complaints. Shamanism fits in neatly with the New Age and self-help movements.

Michael Harner sees a bright future for shamanism. Toward the end of *The Way of the Shaman* he writes:

> The burgeoning field of holistic medicine shows a tremendous amount of experimentation involving the reinvention of many techniques long practiced in shamanism, such as visualization, altered state of con-

---

42   The topic of Soul is discussed in more detail in Section 2-3.

sciousness, aspects of psychoanalysis, hypnotherapy, meditation, positive attitude, stress-reduction, and mental and emotional expression of personal will for health and healing. In a sense, shamanism is being reinvented in the West precisely because it is needed.[43]

Gini Graham Scott, Ph.D., author of *The Complete Idiot's Guide to Shamanism*, writes,

So where is the Shamanism in these modern practices dubbed "Shamanism"? Where is the New Age? Again, they seem almost completely blended together, while the practitioners are using new terms and definitions and claiming ancient links. They are essentially repackaging as Shamanism modern-day teachings about health, wellness, and holistic healing that have been circulating since the 1970s during the heyday of Esalen. That's when the humanistic and transpersonal movements in psychology swept from the West Coast through much of America, and now they seem to have swept up Shamanism, too.[44]

Scott speaks of five branches of shamanism that are current today. One is Traditional Shamanism, which is found in areas untouched by modern influences, e.g., the Asmat tribe of Papua, Indonesia. Second is shamanic practices used for healing and counseling in modern settings often as a business enterprise. Third is the blending of shamanism with medical practices, often using herbs. Fourth is shamanistic journeying techniques employed to contact spirits and other entities. (This is the backbone of Wicca, as will be evident in chapter 3.) Fifth is the blending of shamanistic techniques in journeying and healing methods used in New Age, self-help, and personal

---

43 Harner, *The Way of the Shaman,* 176.
44 Scott, 267-268.

development techniques.[45]

With a big push from the consciousness expanders, whether by way of drugs, the importation of Eastern religious practices, or the study of and experimentation with transpersonal psychology by 'progressives' at Esalen in Big Sur, California, the world of the shaman came to middle America. And it is growing today. Even psychologists and therapists are seeking to treat people through altered states of consciousness, supposing that the worlds imagined in the mind are nothing more than imagination or visualization and are beneficial in working out complex emotional issues. Shamanism, in all its forms, is undergoing a revival.

Shamanistic-based practices are found around the globe. This is so even for people who know little or nothing about shamanism as traditionally understood. Take, for instance, a person in a trance or state of ecstasy, induced by any number of methods, who thereby contacts and has interaction with otherworldly spiritual beings or the spirits or souls of the dead, and then acts as an intermediary for others in performing a variety of duties – this is essentially a shaman, whether he is called a medium, fortune teller, witch, santero, channeler, medicine man, or holy man. David Stern asserts that shamanism is growing, not only in the lands of its origin, Siberia and Mongolia, but in many parts of the world.[46]

Shaman-like persons are found in Buddhism (especially Tibetan Buddhism), Hinduism, Taoism, Shinto, Islam, and Christianity. Though I am a Christian, I am aware that shamanistic influences have also infiltrated parts of Christianity. This will be examined later in the chapter entitled "Charisma: A Surprise Indeed!"

---

45 Ibid., 266.
46 Stern, "Masters of Ecstasy"

CHAPTER TWO

SANTERÍA: FROM SLAVERY TO SLAVERY

After I published a rather brief article dealing with Santería on www.earthenvesseljournal.com a couple of years ago, I received a flood of emails regarding it, some pro but most con. This chapter presents a more in-depth look at Santería, in part to satisfy the requests for more information and also to help answer some of the responses that indicated strong disagreement with my views.[1]

I will admit that my early exposure to Santería was not as thorough as it should have been. Now, however, I am relying on a number of books about the religion, all written by decided proponents, plus personal discussions with a broad spectrum of people. In addition, I have had more time to process what I learned about Santería as I interact with the following sources: (1) *Santería the Religion*, by Migene Gonzalez-Wippler; (2) *Santería: African Spirits in America*, by Joseph M. Murphy; (3) *Santería: The Beliefs and Rituals of a Growing Religion in America*, by Miguel A. De La Torre; (4) *Yoruba-Speaking Peoples*, by A. B. Ellis; (5) *Kingdoms of the Yoruba, 3rd ed.*, by Robert

---

1   Santería is also referred to as La Regla de Ocha or The Way of the Saints. In Cuba Santería is known as Lucumi, in Brazil it is Candomblé or Macumba, and in Puerto Rico, the Dominican Republic, Trinidad, Mexico, and other Latin American countries, it became known as Santería. In Haiti the magical rites are called Voodoo, Vodou, or Voudun. Other names given the religion or systems associated with it are Espiritismo, Curanderism, and Palero.

S. Smith; (6) *The Good The Bad and The Beautiful: Discourse about Values in Yoruba Culture*, by Barry Hallen; (7) article from *Gay Religion* edited by Scott Thumma and Edward R. Gray, entitled "Sexuality and Gender in Santería: LGBT Identities at the Crossroads of Santería Religious Practices and Beliefs" by Salvador Vidal-Ortiz; and (8) many articles that came up in a Google search on the term "Santería," which represented varying points of view.

The sub-title for the chapter, "From Slavery to Slavery," did not come easily. While I attempt to be as accepting and tolerant of other belief systems as possible, the conviction retained after my research was one not likely to be appreciated by those who identified with Santería. The religion promises its adherents freedom but succeeds only in bringing them into spiritual, emotional, and mental bondage comparable in some ways to the devastating slavery that first brought West Africans to the New World. Religion can be healthy and good, but it can also be bad – toxic, cultic, and dangerous. The following description of the basic facts and tenets of this religion may enable readers to make a decision for themselves regarding the nature and value of the religion.

A BRIEF HISTORY OF THE WORSHIP OF THE ORISHAS

Some say the roots of what came to be called Santería in the New World lie in Egypt, Greece, Rome, or even medieval Europe. But certainly it goes back to West Africa, primarily in what are now the nations of Togo, Benin, and Nigeria. The Yoruba people, who settled in these regions about A.D. 1000, had a belief system that brought together many strains of animistic concepts and which resulted in a coherent religious world view. Animism is the belief that "spirits" inhabit the earth in its rocks, plants, streams, animals, mountains, and valleys – indeed all that is natural – and that these can be appealed to, interfered with, communicated with, defended against, and manipulated. Animism is the foundation for many of the world's religions, and this is especially true of Santería.

Olodumare is the name usually given to the one supreme god or "orisha" of Santería. Olodumare is almighty and the source of life. All things are said to come from him, and to him all things are to return. In a way, the doctrine combines monotheism – a belief in one god – and monism – one supreme being who is the *all*. Various "Patakis"[2] of the orishas (also known as Santos), which are stories of the gods and goddesses of the Yoruba religion, including Olodumare, remind one of the foibles of the ancient Greek deities who combined both divine and human traits.

Olodumare is said to be incarnated into the world through "ashé," a creative force, energy, or power that may be obtained by worship and sacrifice to the orishas.

African Slaves Brought to the New World

In 1511, the first African slaves were brought to Cuba from Hispaniola, which is present day Haiti and the Dominican Republic, and these African slaves brought the orishas with them. Starting in 1521, African slaves were transported directly to Cuba where they worked producing primarily sugar and coffee.

Practitioners of Santería who arrived in Cuba were under pressure to hide their Yoruba religious concepts, so they learned to mask or merge their faith with that of the Roman Catholic Church. Already in place in that church was the concept of the immortality of the soul, which led to prayers and offerings made to the dead. The churches were full of carved and painted images of departed people who had been declared saints, but who could, if handled rightly, grant requests. Masking the Yoruba deities with the Catholic saints was a means of keeping the old religion alive, even if it meant attaching names

---

2   A Pataki, of which there are thousands, are tales of the gods of Santería, the orishas.

of saints to the orishas. Catholicism was the seedbed for the survival of the orishas.

The Catholic Church allowed ethnic associations – Cabildos – to form and develop, wherein African dancers worshipped before Catholic images, mostly the Virgin and the older saints. This, combined with the blindness of clergymen who did not understand what they were seeing, made certain that the West African slaves could keep their religious and cultural identity intact.

It was not exactly a form of syncretism, because the belief systems were not combined or inter-twined; rather Spanish Catholicism was a cover to continue worshipping the old gods and goddesses without upsetting or alarming the Catholic hierarchy.

The Yoruba practitioners identified each orisha or Santo with a Catholic saint. *Obatala* became known as Our Lady of Ransom (the virgin Mary); *Eleggua* with Anthony of Padua, Martin of Porres, Benito, the Holy Infant of Prague, and the Holy Child of Atocha; *Orunla* with Francis of Assisi, St. Phillip, and St. Joseph; *Chango* with St. Barbara, St. Mark, St. Jerome, St. Elijah, St. Expeditus, and St. Bartholomew; *Ochosi* with St. Norbert, St. Albert, St. Hubert, St. James; *Oggun* with St. Peter, St. James (in Santiago), St. John the Baptist, St. Paul, the Archangel Michael; *Babalu-Aye* with Lazarus; *Yemaya* with Our Lady of Regla; *Oshun* with Our Lady of Charity; *Oya* with Our Lady of Candelaria, St. Teresita; *Osain* with St. Sylvester, St. John, St. Ambrose, St. Anthony Abad, St. Joseph, St. Benito; *Aganyu* with St. Christopher, Archangel Michael (in Santiago), St. Joseph; *Oko* with St. Isidro; *Inle* with Angel Raphael; *Obba* with St. Rita of Casia, St. Catalina of Siena, the Virgin of Carmen; *Ibeyi* with Sts. Cosmas and Damian, Sts. Crispin and Crispinian, Sts. Justa and Rufina – the heavenly twins.[3] Devotion to and worship of the orishas was carried out beneath the images of the Catho-

---

3   The orisha Ibeyi was connected with twins and thus the saints so identified with Ibeyi would be twins as well.

lic saints, despite the fact that the Church did not endorse or embrace the Yoruba orishas. Sometimes the African religion was opposed; at other times, it was simply ignored.

The numbers of the orishas are variously reported. In West Africa it is probable the number was in the thousands. In the New World that number shrank considerably to 401 according to some and two or more dozen by others. The list above at least names the most popular of the orishas.

The Yoruba people became known as the Lucumi in Cuba, and then as the religion was folded into Spanish Catholicism, the new identity was Santería – loosely translated as "that saint thing." (In Cuba the orisha religion is still known as Lucumi.)

Even Jesus was brought into the Old World religion, given new definitions, roles, and personhood, and became known as *Olofi*. The orisha worshippers cleverly, necessarily, adapted to a strange and hostile environment and succeeded in preserving their gods and forms of worship. In this way they were able to resist being completely subsumed by the European majority.

To survive, then, the Yoruba slaves created a seeming alliance with the dominant religion. The Spanish Catholic Church did not demand doctrinal adherence to or an understanding of its doctrines. Usually the "converts" became so under duress, with hundreds merely sprinkled with holy water – sometimes while still wearing their chains.[4]

African slaves were dispersed thoughout the region – Puerto Rico, the Dominican Republic, Haiti,[5] and to other nations of South America, most notably Brazil (which has a high concentration of those who belong to the orisha religion), Venezuela, and other countries.

---

4   The Church at the time and for a long period afterward did require the slaves to be baptized; but now that Jews, Muslims, and people of other faiths are joining Santería, the requirement to receive Catholic baptism is being abandoned.

5   Due to French influences it is known there as Voodoo or Voudun.

In 1959 and the revolution under Fidel Castro, hundreds of thousands refugees fled from Cuba to the United States, principally to Miami and New York. In 1980, another flood of orisha worshippers was pushed off the island. Now most American cities with any sizable Hispanic population are host to those who keep the worship of the ancient African deities alive.

Compared to the Catholics, the Protestants were not as welcoming to the Yoruba orishas. Membership in Protestant churches was more clearly defined and regulated. Mere baptism was not enough. Doctrine mattered, as did a commitment to Scripture, which had a decidedly negative view of idol worship and occult practices. The Protestant denominations presented a narrow gate rather than the wide gate of Catholicism. Catholicism required little of the slaves beyond attendance at the sacraments. Indeed, "the Catholicism of colonial Cuba was perhaps not so terribly unlike the religion of the Yoruba homeland."[6]

THE THREE "WAYS" OF SANTERÍA

Santería has three basic approaches to the world of the spirits: One, the way of *values* – by honoring ancestors or the "egun;" Two, the way of *power* – direct relationship with spiritual beings, the orishas; Three, the way of *order* – by way of fortune telling or divination.

First is the way of *values*. Here the spirits of the dead are sought to provide ashé. Ashé gives the worshipper power to accomplish and attain things – health, wealth, and power over circumstances and enemies. The ancestors called egun, the people of heaven, provide moral ashé or right behavior. By speaking to the living through one mounted or possessed by the egun, advice and counsel are given. However, the information communicated from the dead to the living is not moral in the traditional sense in terms of right and wrong behavior.

6   Joseph M. Murphy, *Santería: African Spirits in America*, 114.

Ashé from ancestors, or orishas for that matter, may be sought for protection in criminal activity – protection from harm from enemies or the police, or for acquittals in criminal court cases. The egun may prescribe means by which opponents or enemies may be overcome or harmed.[7]

Dead ancestors are said to reincarnate and be born into their original families after two generations minimum. For instance, grandparents' souls might be reincarnated into their grandchildren.

The concept of the immortality of the soul and its transmigration is central to Santería. The doctrine of humans having an immortal soul, but not the idea of a transmigration of that soul, was borrowed from Spanish Catholicism, a doctrine which entered the Church in the fourth and fifth centuries through the writings of Augustine of Hippo, who was deeply influenced by Greek dualistic philosophy that posited the concept of the pre-existent soul and its transmigration.[8]

Second is the way of *power* through orishas who are personifications of ashé that people who honor them can use. In West Africa the lists of the orishas, or gods and goddesses, number about 1700. In the New World the number shrank to either 400 or 401, depending on one's source of information, but in practical reality in contemporary Santería there are seventeen orishas that are worshipped:[9] Obatalá, Elegguá, Orúnla, Changó, Ochosi, Oggún, Babalú-Ayé, Yemayá, Oshún, Oyá, Osain, Ósun, Aganyú, Oko, Inle, Obba, and Ibeyí. The religion

---

7   La Santa Muerte - A Spanish phrase used for a subset of Santeríans notably the Hispanic drug cartels - means the holy dead and the rites and rituals are employed to prosper criminal activity.

8   Augustine rejected, however, the pre-existence of the soul and did not embrace reincarnation, but he did retain the idea of an immortal soul, which has remained a core doctrine for many Christians from that day to this. Biblically speaking, people are soul, in that they are created in the image of God and thus have a relationship with Him. Thus, humans are soul rather than having a separate entity identified as the soul.

9   Some lists have sixteen orishas, others have eighteen.

teaches that priests and priestesses of Santería learn how to make the orisha's ashé available for those who consult them, thus helping them with their lives, or so they understand. In a celebration known as "bembe," the orishas will mount or possess dancers; it is when the dancer is possessed that the power of the orishas is present and may be dispensed to other worshippers.

Also, the worshipper can obtain ashé by sacrificing to the orisha; the sacrifice is known as an "ebbó." The proper sacrifice is determined by divination, performed by the priests, priestesses, and high priests of Santería, respectively the santero, santera, or "babalawo." An orisha may demand an animal sacrifice to obtain the animal's blood, which when sprinkled or poured on an object – usually a sacred stone called the "otane" – it "feeds" the orisha, who then bestows ashé for performing the wishes of the worshipper.

Third is the way of *order*, which has to do with "ifá," or the oracle, the means of divining the future. This may be done by casting, throwing, or dropping palm nuts, cowrie shells, or pieces of coconut on a special flat surface. The babalawo, a higher level of priest, may use a special necklace-like chain that is thrown and then interpreted. For most of the history of Santería, only the babalawo could perform this pinnacle of divination, but in more recent times this is done more and more by the santeros and santeras.[10] The diviner, through whatever means of divination, receives communication from the orisha that "mounted" or possessed him or her at their initiation ceremony, or "asiento," then passes on whatever prescription is the necessary action or remedy to be taken by the worshipper. Nearly all the sacrifices of Santería that are offered to the orishas are a result of divination.

---

10 The Babalawos, the most respected of all the Santería priests, were called the "fathers of the mysteries." It is said that it took ten to fifteen years for a babalawo to learn the art of divination.

Santería and the Cultural Anthropologist

Cultural anthropologists study ethnic groups in order to understand the dynamics of that people group. These scientists do not make value judgments on the political and religious institutions they find. The beliefs and practices of a tribe or culture are merely interesting with no moral evaluation involved; anthropologists do not make a point of assessing the truth or fiction or moral correctness of a religious system.

The African slaves courageously and ingeniously kept their community intact by various mechanisms, not least of which was their belief and worship of the orishas. I am not a cultural anthropologist; thus my evaluation of Santería will not be so sanitized, which should come as no surprise. However, one can admire the history of this religion and its people for their survivability, resistance to extinction, and courage to struggle against the crushing impact of slavery and poverty experienced in the New World.

Spiritism

Spiritism or Espiritismo, which is primarily the concept that the dead live on and may be contacted, impacted Santería in the nineteenth century through the writings of Hippolyte Leon Denizard Rivail, better known by his pen name, Allan Kardec. Born in 1804 in Lyon, France, he became interested in a strange quasi-scientific phenomenon that was sweeping the upper classes of America and Europe called "spirit-tapping." In 1848, the Fox sisters of Hydesville, New York, began experiencing what they thought were the sounds and sights of spirits of the dead attempting to communicate with the living. A quest to explain such phenomena ensued, and it later resulted in something akin to séances led by mediums – those with special talent for contacting the dead.

Santería was ripe to be captured by spiritism. The main tenets of spiritist doctrine are the following:

1) There is a God, defined as "The Supreme Intelligence and Primary Cause of everything." (Easily fits the God concept of Santería.)

2) There are spirits, all of whom are created simple and ignorant, but owning the power to gradually perfect themselves.

3) The natural method of this perfection process is reincarnation, through which the spirit faces countless different situations, problems, and obstacles, and needs to learn how to deal with them. (The egun of Santería visit the living and pass on knowledge of how to learn and perfect themselves. The living are thought to be able to help the egun to learn, grow, and advance in spiritual knowledge and ability.)

4) As part of nature, spirits can naturally communicate with living people, as well as interfere in their lives. Many planets in the universe are inhabited.

5) To accomplish contact with spirits, Allan Kardec's movement, often called Mesa Blanca, began using small groups of mediums to assist in the communicating. This worked perfectly into the thought system of Santerían people. The egun could be contacted by their own mediums, the initiated santeros and santeras, who would be mounted by the orishas. Over time, the old practices from Africa used to contact the egun have been set aside, and the common practices of contemporary mediums have been substituted. The spiritualistic séances, at minimum, have supplemented the way of the orishas.

Thus, all fell into place: The orisha worship of Africa folded into a Catholic setting and was then impacted by American and European spiritism.

THE STRUCTURE, RITUALS, AND CEREMONIES OF SANTERÍA

SANTEROS AND SANTERAS, THE PADRINOS AND MADRINAS – AND THE ILÉ

More and more women, probably now numbering more than men, act as priestesses of Santería. The santeros and santeras are the ones who conduct the asiento or initiation into the religion. All those who are initiated become a member of that santero's or santera's *house* or "ilé." The egun, the dead belonging to the members of the ilé, are also a part of that household.

The priests and priestesses of Santería live for the orishas and help those who seek the aid of the orishas. Santeros, male priests, may be known as Padrinos (godfather) and santeras, female priests, may be known as Madrinas (godmother).

Some long-standing members of Santería complain about how ill-equipped or uneducated many santeros and santeras are. In times past, the time spent in learning the mysteries was long and complex. Now, some are initiated after only a few months.

People in need of help come to the santero priests and santera priestesses to seek a solution to a problem – maybe involving health, money, or love – the top three categories. The price or fee is the "derecho," meaning "right" in Spanish,[11] supposedly limited to covering the price of procuring the items essential for whatever sacrifice might be required by the orisha so that the ashé of the orisha can be secured to resolve the problem. However, apparently prices are going up, and there is a fear that the priests and priestesses are taking advantage of

---

11 As in English, this Spanish word allows several meanings: straight and upright, right side as opposed to left side, human right, and a right determined by law. Perhaps more than one of these meanings is incorporated in Santería but usually refers to the right price asked by the santero or santera.

their very powerful place in the life of their ilé.

There is no actual hierarchy in Santería, no actual organization beyond the ilé. The leader is the santero(a), though the head of all Santería is known as the "Ooni," who is the spiritual head of the Yoruba of Nigeria and of all who worship the orishas in the Americas. The Ooni is said to be a direct descendant of the original persons who founded the Yoruba nation.

Increasingly there is talk of abuses of various sorts being perpetrated on the houses by the "oriate," masters of Santerían ceremonies, the babalawos, and priests and priestesses. These abuses fall into the financial and sexual category. Members of a patrino's or madrina's house become dependent on them to perform certain functions, mostly to secure health, wealth, and romantic issues. And these cost money, often considerable amounts of money.

As a result of the dozens of emails I have personally received from babalawos in particular, in response to YouTube videos I have made or articles on Santería that are published in earthenvesseljournal.com, I am accused of upsetting their business and costing them money. This is increasingly coming to the attention of the ranks of faithful Santeríans. Initiation into the religion may cost tens of thousands of dollars.

Sexuality plays no small part in Santería and its offshoots. There is virtually no moral ethic articulated in any literature produced in Santería, with only the values of a particular culture in which Santería may be found informing the conscience. From what I have read and understood by direct contact, homosexuality and other illicit forms of sexuality are practiced but out of sight of the non-believing world. Between the financial and sexual irregularities, the houses and temples of Santería are being tarnished.

HOW ONE ENTERS SANTERÍA

An initiate is referred to as an "iyawo." The padrinos and madrinas oversee the initiation process. The beginning stage requires one year and seven days, during which time the iyawo wears white clothing, refrains from sexual activity, and learns the way of the saints. The end process is the asiento, when the orisha determined by a babalawo[12] by means of divination mounts the head, or possesses, the iyawo. The asiento, or initiation ceremony, is conducted by a babalawo or an oriate, those who are knowledgeable about Santerían ceremonies. (A further description of the initiation follows.)

There are four requisite roles or steps for a person entering Santería. Each step requires a separate ritual be conducted and results in increasing degrees of protection, power, and knowledge. Full entrance requires reaching all four levels, but a person can stop at any one. The steps or roles are:

1) Receiving "elekes" – the beaded necklaces
2) Receiving the "elegguá"
3) Receiving the "warriors"
4) Making saint or "asiento"

ELEKES

Elekes are beaded necklaces made of different colors and patterns that correspond to the preferences of the orisha of the santero or santera who conducts the initiation.

A babalawo, by the use of a divination ritual called the "bajar a Orunla" determines which orisha(s) will be the initiate's, or "iyawo's" ruling head.[13] The iyawo is usually given four to six necklaces, and removes them only in certain circumstances – bathing, sexual activities, sleeping, and during

---

12 The function of diviner is in more recent times carried out by the padrino (santero) and madrina (santera).

13 Iyawo means "bride of an orisha." A spiritual kind of marriage occurs when an initiate goes through the initiation process and is "mounted" by an orisha at the Asiento.

a woman's menstruation. Breaking a necklace for any reason is a serious problem, and further rituals must be conducted to ward off evil consequences falling upon the owner of the necklace.

The necklaces are given by a "madrina," a santera who officiates or orchestrates the initiation. A derecho or fee is required for this ritual, and it is usually substantial.

The main purpose of the elekes is for protection against all manner of evil, from curses to illnesses. The ashé of the orishas Eleggua, Obatala, Oshun, Yemaya, Chango, and Oya is in the necklaces and is the means of the protection.

RECEIVING OR MAKING ELEGGUA

Eleggua is a "warrior" orisha and is responsible for determining the destinies of people.[14]

A babalawo is consulted, and by using a divining tool like seashells, the initiate's past, present, and future are revealed. From such divining the babalawo prescribes both the building materials and the method for how an image of the head of the orisha Eleggua is to be constructed. The image, mostly made of stones, is then placed somewhere in the house of the iyawo, as close to the front door of the dwelling as possible, in order to protect the house and those living in it from evil forces.

If, for example, a particular person is causing trouble, that person's name is written down on a slip of paper and placed under the image. This assures that the orisha Eleggua will suppress that person from causing evil effects.

The stone image of Eleggua must then be "fed" periodically to assure that there is enough ashé available. This feeding requires blood from a sacrificed animal be sprinkled on the image. In addition to the blood, the image can be fed with the orisha's favorite offerings: rum, cigars, coconut, toasted corn,

---

14 Santería is fatalistic in the sense that a person's future is already determined. However, modifications can be made through magical rituals.

smoked fish, opossum meat, and candy.

Receiving the Warriors

The "warriors," or *guerreros* in Spanish, are given by a babalawo or padrino[15] – the santero or priest who officiates and orchestrates the initiations. The warrior orishas are Eleggua, Oggun, Osun, and Oshosi.

The iyawo now has the protection of Eleggua at this stage, but the protection of the other orishas named above is needed. This overall protection is for battle with enemies, both physical and spiritual.

A distinction in function and power is made between the elekes and the warriors. The elekes are for defensive protection, while the warriors are offensive and attack any who try to do harm.

Making saint or Asiento

Members of Santería will have a pot, a crock, or other receptacle in their house containing the otane stones, collected by means of hearing the voices of the ruling orishas. The stones are, in a sense, the orishas and have within them the ashé of the orishas. The orishas are fed through the stones – they are washed and oiled, and the blood of sacrificed animals is sprinkled on them. The ashé stored in the stones is available for the orishas to then use in assisting those living in the house.

In the asiento – the "ascending the throne" or "making orisha" – the orisha, the identity of which is determined by the babalawo by means of divination, is seated or mounted on or in the head of the iyawo. When this occurs, after a many days-long elaborate ritual, the iyawo may be said to be "born again" into the faith of Santería.

Miguel A. De La Torre has this interesting description of

---

15 The santero and santera, the priest and priestess heads of the ilé, are often now replacing the more honored babalawo's function.

what happens in the asiento:

> Prior to the ritual, the individual is considered impure
> and is therefore required to "die" to their old self.
> The ritual is a process of purification and divination
> whereby the convert becomes like a newborn, even
> to the point of having to be bathed and fed like a baby.
> They are taught the secrets and rites of their god, they
> learn how to speak through the oracles, and they are
> "resurrected" to a new life in which they can unite their
> consciousness with their god. From the moment of the
> asiento, the convert begins a new life of deeper growth
> within the faith.[16]

A person's head is thought to be like a stone, and it is in the
otane stones where the orishas live and their ashé is stored.
A metaphor may be helpful: the stones are like a bank where
deposits and withdrawals are made.

It is said that the iyawo is crowned with the orisha, meaning that the orisha lives in the actual head of the initiate. What
happens as a result of the asiento comes close to the idea of
possession, since the orisha is said to be inside the head of the
iyawo.

Again a quote from De La Torre is helpful in making it clear
what the asiento is:

> The purpose of this ritual is to condition the person's
> mind and body so that all of the supernatural powers of
> their orisha can be invested on the one being ordained,
> allowing him or her literally to become the orisha. This
> ceremony, which requires at least sixteen santeros or
> santeras as witnesses, is also known as an asiento.
> Asiento, the Spanish word for seat, refers to the way in
> which an orisha "mounts" the one being ordained. To

---

16 Miguel A. De La Torre, *Santería: The Beliefs and Rituals of a Growing Religion in America*, 112.

be mounted by an orisha means to be spiritually possessed.[17]

The iyawo or ordained one must observe special conditions for a period of one year, one of which is to abstain from sexual activity for that period. The relationship between human and orisha can be seen as a sexual one – a mystical union in which the orishas are "inside" their brides. They "descend" and "mount" their devotees.[18]

The orisha is said to take over the consciousness of the iyawo, and anything said by the person is now considered to be the direct revelation of the orisha. It is thought that "male orishas spiritually possess female bodies and vice versa."[19] And, "While mounted, the possessed person can predict the future, provide advice, see activities occurring elsewhere, or do anything else capricious gods feel like doing."[20]

In addition to the orisha, the iyawo is also said to be inhabited in the head by an "eleda," said to be a guardian angel.

Making the saint is neither simple nor inexpensive. The ordination process may require as many as three years, though a more contemporary dumbed down version is far shorter. The fee, or derecho, may be as much as $5,000, and some have paid as much as $45,000.

During the feast that follows the asiento, the iyawo is said to be possessed for the first time by their orisha, and at that point a guinea hen's head is removed and the blood is drunk by the iyawo.

For a year following the ordination or asiento, the iyawo

---

17   Joseph M. Murphy, *Santería: African Spirits in America*, 89.

18   Though I have not seen it spelled out clearly, I have found scattered references, in my opinion deliberately obscured, to incubi and succubae - demons that assume human form and have sexual intercourse with humans. It is not clear from the literature if this is what is meant by an orisha mounting the iyawo.

19   De La Torre, 114.

20   Ibid., 115.

learns from their padrino and madrina the fine points of Santería, including the means of fortune telling and how to communicate with the dead.

BEMBE

A bembe is a party,[21] sometimes held out of doors for the public to view, but is most often held at the home, house church, or temple of the santero and/or santera. It is a party filled with African style drumming and dancing.

This is where the heart of the religion takes place. Special dancers and drummers participate. The drums are said to have ashé in them, and that ashé and the praise of the participants – often derisive things said in order to stir up the orishas – make the orishas join the party. The drumming is referred to as "tambor."

It is evident when the orishas show up, as the dancers appear to become possessed and take on the individual orishas' character traits, through styles of dance that are attributed to them. Joseph M. Murphy calls this "a harmony of the human and the divine in dance and joy."[22] The drumming assists in calling the orishas to the party to possess the dancers, who will go into a trance when so possessed.

EBBOS

"Ebbos" are food offerings to the orishas. These may be herbal baths, animal sacrifices, or whatever else may be requested by the orishas through divination.

Ebbos are not bribes, though some are offered to secure the goodwill of an orisha. Ebbos are predominantly for the creation of ashé, that power of the orishas necessary to "help" the petitioner. There are nine different kinds of ebbos, from food offerings to offerings made to make holy the various objects

---

21 Santería has been described as a "dance religion."
22 Murphy, 99.

set aside for offerings.

Candles are lit and various plants are burned, like tobacco in the form of cigars. These offerings are said to release large quantities of ashé. But the amount of ashé released by these is small in comparison to the ashé obtained by means of the blood from animal sacrifices.

According to the religion, the orishas themselves will determine what animals are to be sacrificed and what parts of the animal are to be offered, communicated by way of the priests and priestesses using divination. Some of the animals typically offered are rooster, opossum, pigeon, female goat, white dove, white canary, white chicken, male goat, monkey, sheep, oxen, deer, bull, turtle, rabbit, quail, horse, guinea hen, pig, snake, duck, ram, fish, turkey, owl, and more. The orishas have their favorite animals, which are spelled out in charts but always memorized by the santeros and santeras.

Blood sacrifices are necessary, because the orishas are said to be alive and must therefore eat. The blood of the animals is sprinkled or poured on the stones or otanes, which are the most tangible representation of the orishas on earth. The orishas must be fed, which happens when the blood strikes the stones, thus creating ashé to be used in magic.

There is increasingly less of this kind of ritual in western countries, because people are offended by the animal sacrifices, especially when dead animal carcasses turn up in neighborhoods and other public places. This is part of the effort by Santería to become more acceptable.

SPELLS

Spells and curses are common with Voodoo, but are found in Santería as well. The religion is power-based, controlling and using power for the benefit of practitioners of the faith. For example, for those involved in criminal court cases, a special powder is used to obtain the help of an orisha that specializes in such things. The use of the powder is said to either win a not-guilty verdict or to simply have the subject released from custody. This is why those involved in criminal activity are attracted to La Santa Muerte, "The Holy Dead," a subset of Santería.

An interesting example of a common spell for women in Santería is the following:

> If a woman wishes to seduce a man, she can take seven earthworms, some of her menstrual blood, a dash of her feces, hair from her head and pubic hair, and place them in the sun to dry. When they are dried, she can grind them into a fine powder and place the powder in the man's food or drink.[23]

ADURA

"Adura" is the Yoruba word for prayer, but with a twist. Since some orishas have certain powers which others do not, the proper selection of an orisha to pray to is important. For instance, the orisha Babalu-Aye is best for healing, so those wishing to be healed address the adura to Babalu-Aye.

EWE

"Ewe" are herbs, and they may be a more important component of offerings than an animal sacrifice. Those who deal with herbs, the herb masters, fill the religion's most vital office.

To animists like Santeríans, shamans, Wiccans, and other neo-pagans, plants are alive and have characteristics of personhood, are guarded by certain spiritual entities, and most importantly are loaded with ashé. Herbs are often used as offerings to obtain healing.

Before an herb is used, prayers must be offered that basically ask permission to "take the life of the plant."[24] Once per-

---

23 De La Torre, 128.
24 Ibid., 131.

mission is given, the herb can be used in a variety of ways for medicine or casting a spell or a curse, depending on what the santero or santera desires. An interesting spell used for causing someone to fall in love with another person is the following: A person swallows a few kernels of hard, dry corn. That kernel is retrieved from the feces, washed, roasted, and then ground up into a powder. Then the powder is slipped into the food or drink of the intended love target.

Another fascinating use of ewe, and often employed by practitioners of La Santa Muerte, is the hanging of crabgrass at the four corners of the house where someone wanted by the police is staying. The magic is that the crabgrass somehow disorients the police and no one is found. My favorite is this one: "Washing one's eyes with bog onion is meant to promote clairvoyance."[25]

Since many of the objects necessary for the rituals of Santería are usually obtained in tropical and jungle lands, they are not common in the large cities of the Americas. But specialty stores exist to meet this need. The main place to find all kinds of articles necessary to life in Santería is the "botánica." If one types "botánicas," "pet stores," or "religious goods" into a search engine or consults the yellow pages using these terms, what is revealed is the presence of Santerían retail outlets. These stores will likely incorporate a saint's or orisha's name for easy identification by Santeríans.

OTANES

Otanes are stones that are said to carry within them the actual presence of an orisha and are thus full of ashé. Otanes are carefully selected on beaches, in valleys, on mountains, and so on, and "call out" in some mysterious way to the faithful to be collected.

---

25 Ibid., 133.

The stones are kept in crockery, or a jar of some kind, called a "sopera." The otanes must be fed on a regular basis – with blood at least once a year, periodically refreshed in herbal baths, and oiled with substances as well.

IFA

"Ifa" is the orisha of the oracle, the centerpiece of Santería fortune telling. The babalawo, or more recently the santeros and santeras, "read" the ifa to those who come seeking counsel, healing, and other forms of help. By ifa the priest or priestess of Santería deals with the problems of the community.

Cowrie shells, coconut pieces (four), and palm nuts are thrown, or a chain called the "opele" is laid down and interpreted. Using a strict formula these are "read," and the reading will determine what is to be done about the problem. Doing ifa is the most common of Santería's practices. Essentially, the ifa will reveal if a person is in harmony with his or her destiny, and if not, prescribe what can be done or what offering must be made to bring things back into balance.

MAGIC AND FORTUNE TELLING

What we see when looking at many of the rituals and practices of Santería is simply known as magic. Some of it is fortune telling, and these two, combined with spiritism, make up the three essential branches of the occult. The occult arts are all about acquiring power and knowledge, and knowledge is really power. Some Santeríans will acknowledge this. Others want to disguise it, wanting to give their rituals an identity other than magic and fortune telling, since they are aware that Christianity, including the Catholic Church, declares that occult practices are both non-biblical and dangerous. Christians have always been aware of the power of the occult but ascribe that power to demonic forces.

It is vital to understand the magical, occult nature of

Santería, since the religion must stand as it really is and not on what Santería insiders wish outsiders would not see or know.

PALO MONTE AND PALO MAYOMBE

The Palo sects of Santería originated in the Congo, and developed primarily, but not exclusively, in Cuba. In Spanish it is known as Las Reglas de Congo. In several Caribbean islands, the Congo based system is known as Kumina. Palo means "stick" and is derived from the materials out of which altars were made.

The priests of Palo are called "paleros," and as in the parent body, Santería, they head up houses or temples, which are known as Palo Cristiano. This identification is meant to hide the real nature of the houses and work of the paleros from the dominant Catholicism.

Kardecian spiritism, or Espiritismo, has center stage in Palo Monte. The paleros become possessed by deities and provide advice for members of the Palo Cristiano. This sect is the "dark side" of Santería and is closely tied to black magic and sorcery.

ON WHAT AUTHORITY?

The cultural anthropologist, as previously stated, is not concerned about the authority or truthfulness of a religious system, but many others are, since our interests and concerns go beyond simply describing cultural mores and traits. When one purports to know the will of the supreme deity, others are bound to raise questions and make certain evaluations.

Religions are in competition with one another; they all cannot be correct, since there are significantly different theological and doctrinal views among them. Some are monotheistic, others are monistic, and some are atheistic. The anthropologist need not, as a professional, be concerned about the differences other than to record them.

The question of authority must be raised in regard to Santería and the Yoruba religion of the orishas: What is the authority for the veracity of their religious teachings? How is it that the orisha system is the true paradigm and others are not? Is Santería the truth because a large block of people embrace it? Or, is it truth for only those who are their adherents, which makes each and every religious system nothing more than a culturally unique fantasy devised to explain the human dilemma and ease pain and suffering?

In the Christian Scriptures Jesus said, "I am the way, and the truth, and the life" (John 14:6). Santería teaches that Olofi, an orisha, is Jesus, and that those who worship Olofi are worshipping Jesus. This notion is adverse to true followers of Jesus and is clearly an inauthentic gimmick meant to deceive the unwary.

Christianity has a definite and substantial authority base found in the Bible. The ultimate author of the Book is the Creator God who has revealed Himself in His Son, Jesus Christ. Christianity is a revealed faith; it is either right or wrong, true or false. Christianity and Santería are antithetical – they will not stand together, and any attempt to make them do so is fraudulent.

WHO EXACTLY ARE THE ORISHAS AND THE EGUN?

According to Yoruba traditions the orishas are spirits that have a mysterious power called ashé that must be obtained by the use of praise, sacrifices, and other magical means. Egun are said to be spirits of the dead.

HOW CAN WE BE SURE THIS IS ALL TRUE?

The orishas' behavior reminds us of the antics of the Greek gods and goddesses of antiquity who were capricious, unpredictable, often immoral, even murderous. Many ancient Greeks believed in them but most did not. Greek mythology served people by explaining, in the most crude and unscientific ways, how and why the world existed. The Greek gods were part of fables only and had no actual being. My contention is that this is the same for the orishas and the egun.

The egun, reincarnating from generation to generation, served to comfort people in the face of the reality of death. Death had some of its sting removed through the concept of the immortal nature of the "soul" and its continuous life and contact with the living. While providing comfort and hope is laudable, living with a fictitious world view is not helpful or desirable.

Could the orishas and egun be evil spirits? Many major world religions accept the existence of evil spiritual beings, including Christianity. Christianity posits an evil presence called Satan, who has with him an innumerable number of fallen angels called demons. Satan wanted to be worshipped as God was; this was his undoing and the reason for his ejection from God's presence. Satan craves worship; what a perfect mechanism Santería is for this idol worship!

CONCLUSIONS AND THOUGHTS

As I studied Santeria, the superstitious nature of it jumped out at me. The magical processes that stand at the center of the rituals cannot be ignored by simply taking the cultural anthropologist's way of observing something interesting without attaching moral value to it. To so many, religion is nothing more than a form of theater with no good or bad labels applied.

Beyond the magic, even further to the core of the religion of the orishas is possession, the mounting of the iyawo at asiento, a straight-forward acknowledgment, even goal, of the god or goddess to invade the individual and take that person over. The priests and priestesses of Santería are possessed by gods and goddesses and thus direct other people how to live.

Any slavery is brutal, barbaric, and evil. Evil – the dimensions of evil, the monstrousness of it – will likely only be known to us in some far distant future when its hideous presence has been unmasked and abolished, and the goodness of the Creator God is fully revealed.

This essay is entitled, From Slavery to Slavery. What began with a tribal religion among the West Africans who were transported to the New World and terribly enslaved, morphed into slavery of a different kind, a religion of magic and demonic possession.

Has Santería been beneficial to its adherents? Santería is the means by which the Yoruba culture survived in the New World, but is maintaining ties to that ancient tribal culture worth the cost of trading one kind of slavery for another?

Now, in this present era, Santería is changing to meet the challenges of the post-modern world. The ilés are becoming churches. Men's drumming groups are becoming a means for evangelizing Santería on American college and university campuses. Animal sacrifices are far less common, and the carcasses of dead animals are rarely left for a skeptical public to discover. The wild and implausible stories of the orishas or the patakis are heard and written about much less often. And as De La Torre writes, "The African influences within the religion are minimized as the religion advocates more broadly 'Christian' ethical perspectives and principles."[26]

Santería, due to the fact the religion found itself immersed in a Spanish Catholic world, had to go underground; it had to keep its secrets secret. Understood. But now in a different time and place, Santería means to capture its share of all strata of those hungry for a fuller spiritual life. Indeed, as Miguel de La Torre has so well said, "What was once the religion of the uneducated black lower economic class is becoming the religion of educated middle-class whites."[27]

Santería and shamanism are closely linked, as both depend

---

26 Ibid., 223.
27 Ibid., 224.

upon the trance state or ecstasy. That the same is found in Wicca will be made clear in the next chapter. All are also connected by various occult arts, such as fortune telling and numerous forms of magic. In many of the most crucial ways, shamanism, Santería, and Wicca are virtually identical.

Well-known musical groups today adapt the beautiful and captivating African and Latin drum rhythms and thus open up doors through which new potential converts, largely unsuspecting, are entering. One interesting statistic is that in Brazil, with a population around 190 million people, Santería adherents of various levels may run as high as 90%.

The future will see the institutionalizing of Santería, which will become immediately apparent by typing Santería into a Google search. Right now, Santería has more people devoted to it than many Christian denominations. In fact, it is being viewed now as a world religion alongside Buddhism, Hinduism, Islam, and Wicca. Murphy sees the emergence of Santería and speculates, "We must wait to see where and when the *orishas* may emerge to mount America at large."[28]

Murphy is confident in Santería's ability to win acceptance in America. He looks to the religion's history and sees a story of survival, a miracle in light of the enslavement and removal of a people from the Old to the New World. It is often said that the human tragedy of slavery of the body did not become slavery of the spirit. It is this that I question. Will continued acceptance of Santería bring freedom or slavery?

A look at the teachings and practices of the religion lead me to think that slavery is the answer. Santería, for those who faithfully practice it, will dominate and control most every aspect of their lives. This might seem like a virtue, if the religion was not steeped in magic, fortune telling, spiritism, superstition, and idolatry.

What slavery do I have in mind? Here is a partial list: slav-

---

28 Murphy, 115.

ery to a paranoid mindset where spells and curses are cast and need to be protected against; slavery to the spirits of the dead; slavery to the necessity of placating the orishas and meeting their demands; slavery to a class of priests and priestesses whose very words are to be considered the words of a deity; slavery to the spirits, the saints called orishas, those entities who are in fact nothing more than unclean or demonic spirits.

Finally, practitioners of Santería are determined to display their opposition toward those Christians who challenge their belief systems; I have dozens of emails to substantiate this. Why would this be so? I see their responses to biblically-oriented challenges as fearful, which is because Jesus, and only Jesus Christ of Nazareth, has power and authority over demonic spirits.

During the earthly ministry of Jesus, He cast out demons, and this troubled and amazed the people of His day, including the religious leaders.[29] He also gave His disciples authority to do the same, and they have indeed done so over the centuries. The Apostle John even said, "The reason the Son of God appeared was to destroy the works of the devil" (1 John 3:8). And then James said, "Submit yourselves therefore to God. Resist the devil, and he will flee from you" (James 4:7).

Ultimately the reason for this chapter is to speak a word of grace, peace, and mercy to those entangled in Santería. My intent is also to caution those drawn to Santería: **There is more to it than meets the eye.**

---

29 Reading through the Gospel of Matthew will make this abundantly clear.

CHAPTER THREE

WICCA: WITCHES AMONG US

The neo-pagan religion of Wicca is not coming to a town near you - it is already there! The Unites States government recognizes Wicca as a legitimate religion, and there are Wiccan chaplains in the military and in some state prisons.

Witchcraft, covens, magick, gods, goddesses, spells, curses, astral travel, fairies, elves, dead ancestors, animal guides, and much more exist in the "otherworld." Is it nonsense, game playing, fantasy, a marketing gimmick or, is there some kind of reality behind it? Whatever the answer may be, Wicca is a growing phenomenon and not likely to recede any time soon.

In the previous chapter, we looked at Santería, the West African religion that came to the New World due to the slave trade that flourished from the sixteenth to the nineteenth centuries. The Yoruba tribe of West Africa worshipped deities called orishas. In the New World orisha worship commingled with the Roman Catholicism that was already present in the Hispanic Caribbean Islands. The new religion – really the old Yoruba religion of Africa – became known as Santería (loosely translated into English as "the saint thing"). While researching this transplanted religion, I noticed how much the Santerían world view paralleled that of Wicca. Having then completed a lengthy essay on Santería, which formed the basis of the previous chapter, I purchased a number of books on Wicca hoping to further understand this religion that is growing in popularity, particularly in America.

Note:

Since there is no official document that authoritatively speaks to the central dynamics and principles of Wicca, the following are statements to which most Wiccans seem to subscribe, yet as is often the case, not by all. Out of necessity, they will be somewhat overlapping and even contradictory. My personal commentary on Wicca will comprise the last part of this chapter.

PART I: BASIC FACTS ABOUT WICCA FROM ITS PROPONENTS

» Wicca is a growing religious system, though there is no hierarchical Wicca Church as in Methodists or Baptists. The number of books on Wicca on the market is growing rapidly, and there are more than 6,000 Wicca-related websites on the Internet. There are Wiccan radio shows, Wiccan umbrella organizations, and state-certified Wiccan churches.

» No one knows the origins of witchcraft. Gerald Gardner, the person who more than any other is responsible for bringing the cult into the modern era, said: "My own theory is, that it is a Stone Age cult of the matriarchal times, when woman was the chief; at a later time man's god became dominant, but the woman's cult, because of the magical secrets, continues as a distinct order."[1]

» Judy Harrow, in the foreword to the fiftieth anniversary edition of *Witchcraft today* by Gerald Gardner, attributes a major change for Wicca with the 1979 publications of Margot Adler's *Drawing Down the Moon* and

---

1   Gerald Gardner, *Witchcraft Today*, 43. (Note that Gardner's theory of prehistoric matriarchy is well-disputed. See a fuller discussion in Cynthia Eller, *The Myth of Matriarchal Prehistory: Why an Invented Past Won't Give Women a Future* (Boston: Beacon Press, 2001).

Starhawk's *The Spiral Dance,* wherein the emphasis is on the "joyous worship of Mother Earth."[2]

»   A Wiccan is a person who is following the Wiccan religion/spiritual path and has either undergone a Wiccan initiation or has formally and ritually declared him- or herself Wiccan.

»   Some Wiccans use the words "Wiccan" and "witch" interchangeably, but there are witches who do not consider themselves Wiccans. Wiccans are a subgroup of witches. Wiccans and witches are both subgroups of a larger group: pagans. Pagans are practitioners of earth-based religions. Most Wiccans and witches consider themselves pagan, but not all pagans are Wiccans or witches.

»   *Witchcraft* is what Wiccans and witches do, and "Wicca" is the name of the religion itself. There are a number of groups that are Wiccan. Some of these are: Alexandrian, Celtic, Dianic, Dicordian, Eclectic,[3] Gardnerian,[4] Neo-Gardnerian, and Georgian.

»   A *solitaire* is a witch who practices alone and is not in a *coven.* A coven can vary in size, but 13 is the number of persons who comfortably fit into the ritual circle. In it is the High Priestess, who is seen as the goddess incarnate and is the spiritual center of the coven. Also there may be a High Priest, who assists the high Priestess, and is seen as the god incarnate.

»   Wicca is new but old at the same time. Its origins

2   Judy Harrow, in Gerald Gardner's *Witchcraft Today,* 2004 edition.

3   Here is found a number of Wiccan traditions bound together, and no two groups may be identical. Individual witches, or solitaires, will develop their own practices, rites, and ceremonies.

4   Gerald Gardner was instrumental in focusing modern Wicca. His *The Gardnerian Book of Shadows* describes the major ceremonies and rites of Wicca.

are shrouded in mystery, and many will say it began among rural Celts.[5] Magic – and magic is what Wicca is about – has been practiced since prior to recorded human history. Wiccans spell magic with a "k" - thus, "magick" is the word used.

» The Wiccan path is based on the earth rather than the heavens.

» A witch uses magick in his or her everyday life.

» There is no central church of Wicca, and no Wiccan bible or sacred document exists of any kind that details the beliefs, rules, and teachings of the religion.

» Wiccans are monotheistic.[6] Their primary deity may be referred to as "The All," "The Universe," and "The One." The Lord and Lady, or the god and goddess[7] came from or out of "The All."

» Wicca embraces reincarnation and karma, concepts carried to India in and around the tenth century B.C. and was absorbed into Hindu monistic thought. After a certain degree of westernization, it is for most Wiccans the idea that there is death and rebirth, a process that goes on until balance and perfection are reached.

» There is a male and female aspect of all people; thus there is a natural equality of the sexes. But these aspects are not in balance. A central goal of Wicca is to restore the proper balance.

---

5   *The Oxford Concise English Dictionary* defines "Celt" as: "a member of a group of western European peoples, including the pre-Roman inhabitants of Britain and Gaul and their descendants, especially in Ireland, Wales, Scotland, Cornwall, Brittany, and the Isle of Man."

6   The Wiccan concept of monotheism is not the same as that of Judaism, Christianity, or Islam, where the God of creation, the God of Abraham, Isaac, and Jacob, is the primary and single God.

7   Wiccans capitalize "Goddess" and "God" but I use the lower case.

» Wiccans strive for a balance between the male and the female, and when such a state is reached, reincarnations cease and the individual enters into their version of heaven called Summerland.

» "You learn Wicca by loving it," is a common statement made by Wiccans.

» Wicca, with its focus on natural cycles and its emphasis on meditation and psychic abilities, provides many opportunities to touch the mysteries of the divine and the cosmos.

» Some Wiccans teach that Wicca is European Shamanism: the word *shaman* refers to a person who enters an altered state of consciousness in order to take a spiritual journey to retrieve information, heal, work magick, tell the future, or commune with the dead.[8]

» Wicca is a religion that many (but not all) witches practice. It is an earth-based religion that honors both the god, represented by the sun, and the goddess, represented by the moon.

» Wiccans are taught to be in tune with their psychic abilities. Magick circle, the sacred space of Wiccans, is said to be "between the worlds," and Wiccans "travel" between the worlds to meet the gods, receive information, and heal. Wiccans often enter ecstatic or trance states in order to work magick or commune with the divine.

» Many Wiccans have life-altering experiences that lead them to the Wiccan path, and Wiccan groups often initiate new members in a symbolic death and rebirth

---

8   This particular concept - the altered state of consciousness - figures large in shamanism, Santería, and Wicca, along with a number of other religious or spiritual practices. Another word for the altered state of consciousness is "trance." Trance is particularly important in Wicca.

ceremony meant to provide a mini-shamanic crisis and shift the initiate's perspective.[9]

» Wicca is a magickal system. As generally understood, there are two types of Wiccan magick. (1) There is every day magick. This might consist of spell work for things like finding a new job or protecting one's home. (2) There is magick to manifest or make real the witch's personal power and divinity. In essence, it is a working the witch's will to find purpose in life and alignment with the higher self.

PART II: GENERALIZED STATEMENTS FROM PROPONENTS OF WICCA[10]

» "If you use your magickal[11] energies, they may just help you stay clear-headed and focused. Powers are a special blessing that we all have. Some witches believe that their powers come from the Goddess. Wherever they come from, just know that you have them. If you open your heart and mind, you can use your powers. And the more you work with them the better, the more powerful, you become."[12]

» The abilities you have are natural and inborn, so there is no reason to be frightened of them. Soon you will come to rely on them.

» Nature is never good or evil, it just is. Wicca is often

---

9 The parallels to Christianity are perhaps deliberate but disingenuous.

10 There is a certain redundancy in these statements, since different branches of Wicca and Wiccan writers will describe the core ideas differently. It is necessary to present the overlapping in order to see the full range of Wiccan thought.

11 Magic is what magicians do on the stage, in film, on television; magick with a "k" is what Wiccans do.

12 Zimmermann and Gleason, *Wicca and Witchcraft*, 6.

compared to Native American beliefs and traditions. Witches recognize that it is in our best interests to keep the earth healthy and vital. While many religions have a holy book, our book is the earth itself and all of her creatures.

»   The Goddess and God will take notice [of your attention to them through rituals] and your spells will soar!

»   "Wiccans believe that the Goddess is in everything and is not some force standing *out there* watching us. In the faith of Wicca, we believe in deity – the All. We divide that into a male and female spirituality, the God and Goddess, or Lord and Lady."[13]

»   Wiccans also work with the demigods who are different, smaller aspects of the All.

»   Witches are not anti-Christian, nor do they harbor negative feelings about other religions. Witches will, however, avoid "narrow Christians" and not allow one to be in their ranks.

»   Wiccans deny Jesus is the Son of God but accept Him as an enlightened or holy man.

»   "Wiccans believe in the morals that are common to most faiths. But Wiccans do not believe in the Christian concept of original sin. Wiccans live in the now. While some Wiccans believe in reincarnation, life is to be lived for what it is in the present so that we may learn from this lifetime on Earth. As Wiccans, we do not deny ourselves pleasure or put up with unnecessary pain. We believe that we all have a job to do, or a lesson to learn, or maybe a debt to pay from the last lifetime. Once we have succeeded in our mission, we must move on to the Summerland, where we can reflect and choose our mission in the next life. Or, perhaps choose not to reincar-

13   Ibid., 7.

nate and rather work as spirit guides."[14]

» While Wiccans do not believe there is a hell to punish sinners, they do believe there is a universal law, called *karma*.[15] Witches know that whatever energy or actions they send out, whether negative or positive, they will come back to them *threefold*.[16]

» If you send out positive energies, you will get positive energies in return.

» The central principle of Wicca is the Wiccan Rede, *"An it harm none, do what ye will."*

» Witches do believe in "God," the pure energy of the All, of the god and goddess, most high. Witches do not believe in Satan.

» It's often prudent not to openly broadcast your status as a witch. Spirituality is, after all, a personal affair. If friends are curious, answer their questions honestly but stress the positive aspects of your religion: Harm none; live as though the Earth and all of its inhabitants are sacred; strive toward the positive.[17]

» Wiccans believe that all spiritual paths lead to the same house – union with the divine. Perhaps, in our search for tolerance, harmony, peace, and freedom of spirit, by the end of this millennium all the major religions will have broken down and merged together into one gentle and magickal earth-centered faith.

---

14 Ibid., 11.

15 Unlike the Hindu version of Karma and reincarnation, Wicca employs a watered down version of the two concepts, making them more acceptable to the Western mindset.

16 There will be more on the Threefold Law further in the chapter.

17 There is a tendency of Wiccans to be less than forthcoming about what they actually do and believe. Full disclosure is not common among witches - a mark of a cultic mentality.

PART III: THE WICCAN DEITIES

» In Wicca, the Divine or Deity is greater than creation, and yet it is creation. Deity or the Divine is immanent in all things, but it is also distant and beyond grasp.

» In Wiccan thought, the union of the goddess and god creates the universe. The goddess is the god's mother and lover. In the mythos of most Wiccans, the goddess gives birth to the god, he matures, they make love and she becomes pregnant, he dies, and he is reborn of her again. The god's existence is cyclical, like the grains.

» Communicating directly with the god and goddess is one of the greatest joys and responsibilities of a Wiccan.

» Many Wiccans have personal patron deities - in addition to the god and goddess - with whom they work frequently.

» The Celtic, Greek, Roman, Norse, and Egyptian gods are probably the most popular amongst Wiccans.

» In addition to the god and goddess, a Wiccan may be involved with any number of otherworldly entities. There are, in addition to the personal deities, the animal *familiars*,[18] dead ancestors, gnomes, elves, and so on. It seems there are any number of spiritual entities, not all of the good kind, that hover around Wicca and are involved in casting the spells and conducting the rituals.

» There are two types of Wiccan animal familiars: disincarnate (spirits in animal form) and incarnate (spirits indwelling living pets or other animals). Disin-

---

18 A familiar spirit is one that masks itself as someone familiar to you - a deceased grandparent, for instance. The animal familiar will appear as a dog, cat, or other animal that one is familiar with.

carnate animal familiars or spirits serve as guides and helpers. Not all Wiccans work with animal spirits. In the accounts of the witch trials, there are stories of animal familiars, most of which were said by the witches' accusers to be demons in animal form. Proponents of Wicca strongly believe the animal familiars are not demons. A Wiccan chooses the animal spirits to work with, but it is said that sometimes the animal familiar does the choosing.

PART IV: THE WICCAN RITUAL

» A Wiccan ritual is a means of creating consecrated ground or sacred space in order to pay homage to deity. Ritual is also used to do magick and to work with the energy of the god and goddess.

» It is a good idea to do a small ritual every day to honor the Lord and Lady.

» Rituals can be performed for grounding, to connect with the goddess, to celebrate a *sabbat*, to honor one's ancestors, or to perform magick.

» There are eight sabbats having to do with the earth and the positioning of the sun. These fall about six weeks apart. Four of them are known as solstices and equinoxes, and the mid-points between them are the *cross quarters*.

» Covens meet to perform rituals together regularly – for the thirteen *esbats*, or Wiccan moon rituals, and eight sabbats every year. Esbats have to do with the moon, especially full moons; the sabbats have to do with the sun.

» In the ritual, it is necessary to call down the *quarters* – the four directions of North, East, South, and West – and the Elemental powers of Earth, Air, Fire, and

Water. Over these is spirit, which sits atop the *pentacle.* A pentacle is a pentagram, a five pointed star, with a circle around it.

»   A high priestess will "call down the moon" to give her power to do magick. She is then considered to be an incarnation of the goddess.

»   The circle is drawn with an *athane* (a small, hand-made dagger) to a diameter of nine feet. Another circle is drawn one foot outside that one and even another circle is drawn another one foot outside the second.

»   Once the Powers have been called down or in they must be told or shown what they are to do. Often the Powers are "bound" with a rhyme.

»   Doing magick takes serious and sincere prepara-tion of the body, mind, and spirit on a daily basis and becomes time consuming, even controlling.

»   A witch's journal is called a *Book of Shadows*; a witch's recipe book is called a *grimoire.* The grimoire can also contain lists of angels, spirits, and magickal properties of objects found in nature. Gerald Gardner's *Book of Shadows* has become the standard for all gri-moires.

PART V: SUMMON, STIR, CALL, INVITE, OR REQUEST

»   Wiccans "summon" certain entities – the four ele-ments, fairies, and the *elementals*, for example. The four elements are air, fire, water, and earth. The elementals are personifications of the four elements. The elemen-tal associated with air is sylphs, fire is the salaman-der, water is undines or nymphs, and earth is gnomes. Other larger, more powerful entities are "stirred." These are the Ancestors, dragons, and Watchtowers. One stirs them because they are sleeping and need to be awakened before they can attend the ritual. If one wants the god and goddess to attend one's ritual, "call" them respectfully, and they will come. And one can call angels also. When one "invites" entities to one's ritual, it is asking them to be present, but not to join inside the circle. These are the familiar entities. One can "request" the presence of any of the four winds and of one's spirit guides. Also, one tells the entities asked to the ritual what they are to do. One can ask them to protect, observe, or help carry out one's magick.

ENTITIES:

» Air, Fire, Water, Earth and Spirit have dragons from the Elemental Realm.

» Guardians of the Watchtowers: some witches are afraid of them and won't use them in ritual.

» Fairies: flower fairies, mermaids, mermen, little people, sprites, and pixies. These can appear as miniature humans, or they can take the form of an elf. They are summoned. You'll know that the fairies have arrived when the flames of your candles start to dance around. They are extremely mischievous. To discourage fairies from taking up permanent residence in your home, hang iron pots around the house. Because iron renders fairies powerless and incapable of magick, they will flee from this metal and leave you in peace.

» Elementals: Sylphs, salamanders, undines, and gnomes.

» Tree spirits: from the realm of Fairy.

» The Lord and the Lady: around us all the time. So, too, are all the many varieties of angels. The ancestors also dwell in the Realm of Spirit, but they are sleeping.

» Angels: divided into three levels: One, seraphim, cherubim, and thrones. Two, dominions, virtues, and powers. Three, principalities, archangels, angel messengers, and guardian angels.

» Ancestors: figures from the past who have great wisdom and knowledge. They have lived in the times of Egypt, Rome, or Greece, like Socrates. An ancestor might even be an actual ancestor like a grandparent.

» Spirit Guides: like guardian angels, are assigned to us at birth, and we can have as many as seven. Sometimes a spirit guide is a soul that does not need to be reincarnated. Often spirit guides come to us in our dreams. If you meditate regularly, you may start being able to see them.

» Spirit animals: (disincarnate) may be summoned.

» Familiars: individual animals that are inhabited by spirit (incarnate). They can help with magick. Familiars have more dignity than regular pets because they are able to communicate with you telepathically.

PART VI: BASIC WICCAN PRINCIPLES AND ETHICS

Much of Wiccan practice can be divided into two categories - eclectic and traditional.

Eclectic: This is where Wiccans compile their practices from a variety of sources.

Traditional: Wiccans here use a system of practices that have been handed down to them and have a certain level of consistency, though the lines will sometimes blur. Some of the traditions are: Gardnerian, Alexandrian, Feri, 1734, Celtic and/or Celtic Reconstructionist, Minoan, Seax Wicca, Asatru, Church of All Worlds, Covenant of the Goddess, New Reformed Orthodox Order of the Golden Dawn, Central Valley Wicca, Blue Star, Dianic Wicca, and Reclaiming.

To save time and space, no elaboration will be made here on these traditions, since that is not germane to our purpose.

KEY GENERAL PRINCIPLES

» Wiccan Principle 1: Deity becomes a polarity. Many Wiccans believe that there is a single great divine force, which they call spirit, the All, the Divine, or just Deity.

» Wiccan Principle 2: Deity is immanent, meaning that deity is inherent or present in all people and things. This is close to the definition of animism, which is that everything has a consciousness of its own but different in that there is a sacred force that infuses everything, and that force is deity or a part of deity.[19]

» Wiccan Principle 3: The Earth is divine. Wiccans believe that the earth is a manifestation of deity, and may be called Gaia.[20] Therefore, many Wiccans believe that a significant part of their spiritual path is taking care of the earth.[21]

» Wiccan Principle 4: Psychic power or psychic abilities help Wiccans with many things, like honing their intuition, divination (reading astrological charts or tarot cards, for example), and sensing things that science cannot yet explain, like the spirits of the dead or the presence of the gods with people.

» Wiccan Principle 5: The use and practice of magick

19 The distinction between ancient animism and Wicca's concept of the force or energy in all appears to be but a quibble.

20 Gaia, in Wicca, is a female deity that can be involved in magick and ritual. Gaia theory, the concept of an earth, indeed a universe, that regulates itself in unknown ways, is not a part of Wicca but rather is a scientific theory.

21 Interestingly, Wiccans tend to think that Christians, who believe in a heaven, are not living in the "here and now" and take little interest in the environment.

– the idea that everything is infused with the divine and thus the divine can cause change to occur in conformance with the will of the magickian. Further, it is the concept that all things contain some divine energy, which can be tapped into in order to affect change.

»   Wiccan Principle 6: Reincarnation. Wiccans have at least three different positions on this. (1) Some believe that our souls are reborn into new bodies. (2) The human essence "recycles" after the body dies and becomes cosmic energy. (3) All humans share one soul, and this soul experiences the many possibilities of life by inhabiting all of our bodies at the same time.

»   Wiccan Principle 7: Sex is sacred, sexuality is then considered a gift from the gods, and gay sex is as good as any other form of sex, except that none are to be harmed in the practice of sacred sex.

KEY ETHICAL PRINCIPLES

»   Wicca is not Satanic or anti-Christian. Wiccans do not believe in Satan. Satan is part of the Christian religion, and Satanism is a Christian heresy.

»   Wiccans do not try to convert others to Wicca.

»   Wicca is not dualistic, as in a good god fighting with a bad god. Wicca does not see God and Satan as opposite partners, or two parts of a whole.

»   Wiccans can honor more than one religion.

»   Wicca is not a way to get power over others, not only about magick, not an excuse to wear edgy clothes, nor is it a mask for sexual abuse.

»   Witches should never attack, but they can use their magick to defend themselves.

»   Do no harm. Everything else is fair game.

» "Black magic" – magick is like electricity. It is neither good nor bad. It just is. If you intend to harm, you are doing negative magick. If you intend the greatest good for all, then you are working positive magick.

» All things in life exist along a continuum. Our actions are neither totally good nor totally bad, but lie somewhere between these two polarities.

» Are life forms killed in a healing, let us say, when germs are poisoned by antibiotics? Everything has a right to live. But a virus or bug is making someone sick, and a healing is therefore justified. The point is that the greater good predominates.

PART VII: THE THREEFOLD LAW

Many, but not all, Wiccans subscribe to the Threefold Law. This law teaches that whatever you put out into the world or universe will come back to you three times. And this may be good or bad.

This concept is based on the principle of "like attracts like." The goal, therefore, is to put out positive energy and not negative energy. It is not necessarily dealing with good or bad behavior, since that would begin to evolve into rule-setting and then performance of that which was good and avoidance of that which was bad.

When the Threefold Law and the Rede, "An it harm none, do what ye will," are taken together, you see that if you are working your true will, if you are synchronized with the universe and the divine, then the positive energy you generate ripples out and affects everything around you, and it is a beacon for other positive energy to be attracted to you. This is the place where Wiccans strive to be.

PART VIII: SUMMERLAND

Summerland beckons. It is not heaven and it is not hell.

Some witches believe it is where spirits go after death to rest and reflect in the company of the god and goddess, and to decide how they are going to reincarnate. Each soul chooses who it will be and what lesson it will learn in its new lifetime. Once it is reincarnated, it does not remember what its lesson is, but must find out by living through all the experiences of its new life. If a soul does not wish or need to reincarnate right away, it may become a spirit guide. Ultimately, each spirit, after it has learned all it needs to learn and taught what it needs to teach, is reunited with the All. In each lifetime, the spirit advances toward this ultimate goal.

Though Wiccans believe that all animals have souls, these do not go to Summerland, since the souls of animals are so pure they have no lessons to learn in this life.

PART IX: WHAT IS ENERGY IN RELATION TO DEITY, AND WHAT IS VISUALIZATION?

For some Wiccans, "energy" and deity are the same thing. Some Wiccans refer to energy and deity as the "life force." Others see deity as sentient, thus having consciousness and the capacity to experience things as humans do with their senses. Still others think that energy emanates from deity, or that it comes from the goddess.

Others will say that energy is power, and that of three types: personal power, divine power, and earth power.

"Visualization" is the creating of a picture in the mind's eye of what it is the magickian wants to happen. Once visualization occurs, energy follows thought. If you can see something in your mind, then you can affect it or make it happen.

PART X: TRANCE AND PATHWORKING

Trance is integral to the religious or spiritual practices discussed in this book and is the centerpiece of each of them, no more so than with Wiccan practice. It is at this point that we present Ioan M. Lewis' work on trance and ASC.

Ioan M. Lewis is a Fellow at the British Academy and Professor Emeritus of Anthropology at the London School of Economics, UK and author of "The Social Roots and Meaning of Trance and Possession" in the *Oxford Handbook of The Sociology of Religion*, edited by Peter B. Clarke and published by Oxford Press in 2009.

The opening sentence in the Oxford Handbook on Lewis' contribution is: "Altered States of Consciousness' (ASC) is an umbrella term, applied to psychological and sociological phenomena regularly encountered in the study of trance, possession, and shamanism – all of which have significant if problematic links with music."[22]

"Music" – a surprise? No, since in Santería there is the bembe with the bata drumming, shamanism with much the same, Wicca and the mood music, then charisma with the beat of the drum and the bass guitar. A strange connection? Not really.

There is more beyond the music. Dancing of a certain kind goes with much of the music and is present in all four of the spiritual practices above. The impact of music, dancing, singing, chanting, and other stimulants is such that even the chemical make-up of the brain can be altered. Below is a paragraph from Lewis that summarizes his thesis:

> Such personal, psychological experiences may, of course, be shared and mutually intensified as in spirit cult séances, evangelical religious services, pop concerts, political rallies, football crowds, etc. The discovery of natural euphoriates (endorphins) in the bloodstream in the early 1970s provided a plausible chemical explanation of trance, and linked it with the effect of psychotropic drugs, thus giving a novel and unexpected meaning to Marx's famous definition of

---

22 *Oxford Handbook*, 375.

religion as "the opiate of the people"--more accessible and less mysterious than he ever imagined.[23]

Lewis condenses entering into the trance to two processes: sensory deprivation and sensory overloading. Deprivation is by means of trauma, stress, illness, isolation, fasting, and submission to physical pain. Overloading is by means of "musical and other sonic bombardment (especially monotonous drumming), strobe lighting effects, the ingestion of hallucinogenic drugs, and more mundane procedures like over-breathing and even strenuous exercise."[24]

This semi-scientific explanation of the induction of a trance state may be, in my estimation, somewhat limited but is nevertheless sufficient. The shaman and Wiccan understand that the ultimate purpose for the trance is to have a spirit or other ethereal entity enter the body of the person entranced. This possession marks the real initiation for the person entering into the priesthood of Santería, authenticates a person as a true shaman, and demonstrates the authority of the witch. In charisma the sudden change in behavior or appearance of the "anointed one" signals that a "prophet" or "prophetess" is present to heal or utter a "thus saith the Lord." It is the trance that makes the difference. As Lewis puts it, "Trance is cross-culturally the most conclusive public demonstration that a human being has been seized by a spirit."[25]

There can be a sexual component to the trance state. Lewis points out that St. Teresa of Avila "recorded that in her transports of mystical feeling she had achieved 'spiritual marriage' with Christ. Her most sublime experiences she described as unfolding in three stages: 'union', 'rapture', and the climatic 'wound of love.'"[26] In a parallel way shamans will consider they

---

23 Ibid., 378.
24 Ibid.
25 Ibid., 383.
26 Ibid., 382. In other research we have received testimony from per-

are "bound in marriage" to the orisha, god or goddess, that has mounted them at their initiations. Lewis points out the "pervasiveness of eroticism in describing the relations between humans and spirits."[27]

Lewis concludes and reconnects with his opening theme by stating, "In this sensual perspective, although the precise modalities of music and trance seem still imprecisely defined, music is nevertheless evidently the food of love."[28]

If music, what then of dance? In Judy Harrow's section in the back of *Gardner's Witchcraft Today,* she quotes Doreen Valiente, one of Gardner's High Priestesses:

> Dancing has a very important magical effect upon people. . . . A group of people dancing in harmony together are on one mind, and this is essential to magical work. Their mood can be excited or calmed by varying the pace of the dance. In fact, a state of light hypnosis can be induced by magical forms of dancing; or people can achieve a state of ecstasy, which in its original form is ex-statis, "being outside oneself."[29]

Harrow goes on to say that since Gardner's time dance has increased in popularity; indeed, a new movement "called Sacred Circle Dance, which uses rhythmic bodily movement to alter consciousness..."[30] is widely practiced.

Dr. Margaret Murray, former assistant professor in Egyptology at University College, London, who wrote the Witchcraft entry for the 1929 edition of the *Encyclopedia Britannica* and is one of the early proponents of paganism, also noted the

---

sons who experienced sexually-oriented trances in which spirit beings, especially animal helpers, actually have sexual intercourse with those they possess.

27 Ibid., 386.
28 Ibid.
29 Gardner, *Witchcraft Today*, 178.
30 Ibid., 179.

role of music and dance in pagan worship:

> All the movements are rhythmic, and the accompani-
> ment is a chant or performed by percussion instru-
> ments by which the rhythm is strongly marked. The
> rhythmic movements, the rhythmic sounds, and the
> sympathy of numbers all engaged in the same actions,
> induce a feeling of exhilaration, which can increase to
> a form of intoxication. This stage is often regarded by
> the worshippers as a special divine favour, denoting the
> actual advent of the Deity into the body of the worship-
> per.[31]

Pathworking depends upon the trance state. Trance states
can be reached by any number of ways. Attempts at centering, balancing, grounding, relaxing, focusing on a single object,
letting the mind wander, emptying the mind of all – these are
some of the mechanisms commonly used to enter into trance.
Drugs can be used, and extreme experiences such as in a sweat
lodge, reduction of oxygen coming into the brain, and other
esoteric practices can be employed.

Once in the trance state, the pathworking can begin.
Along the path, helpful guides may be encountered whom
the entranced individual can ask for information. Likewise,
one's inner self (supposedly the personification of the sub-
conscious) may be encountered. Or an animal or human spirit
that is associated with a sacred site may be found. Also, path-
working can be used to meet with, talk to, and get information
from the dead.

The advice given to one doing pathwork is to be polite to
any being encountered, be they human spirits, gods, fairies,
elves, animal spirits, ghosts, folklore characters, or other entities. Wiccans deny that there is any danger in being in a trance,
but do assert that a person in the trance state is more vulnera-

---

31 Gardner, *Witchcraft Today*, 15-16.

ble to "ambient"[32] energies, because the conscious mind, which would normally trigger you to tune out unwanted energy, sounds, or other distractions, is on a little vacation when you are in trance.

PART XI: GERALD GARDNER AND WICCA

In Gerald Gardner's, *The Gardnerian Book of Shadows*, is described the "Eightfold Path or Ways,"[33] which reveals Wiccan dependence on the trance state.

One of the most respected Wiccans, a co-founder of Reclaiming, is Starhawk, who writes, "Witchcraft is a shaman-istic religion, and the spiritual value that is placed on ecstasy is a high one. It is the source of union, healing, creative inspi-ration, and communion with divine."[34] The Eightfold Path is a way to lead a person to the "center" and to leave one's body by means of a trance, or altered state of consciousness, or by what Michael Harner would call the Shamanic State of Con-sciousness, SSC.

- » Path 1: Meditation or concentration
- » Path 2: Trance states, clairvoyance, projection of the Astral
- » Path 3: Drugs, Wine, Incense
- » Path 4: Dance, Performing Rites with a purpose
- » Path 5: Chants, Spells, etc.
- » Path 6: Blood control (Cords etc), Breath control

---

32 Ambient here means energies, specifically supernatural entities, that might happen to be nearby and might not be friendly, might even be nasty. Wiccans would not describe these as being evil.

33 Gerald Gardner, *The Gardnerian Book of Shadows*, Forgotten Books, 2005, 65. Gardner was born in 1884 and died in 1964. His craft name was Scire.

34 Starhawk, in *Gay Religion*, from the essay by Mary Jo Neitz entitled "Queering the Dragonfest: Changing Sexualities in a Post-Patriarchal Reli-gion," edited by S. Thumma and E. R. Gray, Altamira Press, 2005, 272.

> » Path 7: Scourge
> » Path 8: The Great Rite

The first six paths are fairly plain as to their nature; however, number 7 and 8 require some explanation.

The Scourge is a magickal tool used to direct spiritual entities and is used inside the circle. It is a whip or flail and can be used to flagellate members of the coven, especially in initiation rites. Symbolically it stands for suffering and sacrifice that one is willing to endure.

The Great Rite is a form of sex magick that may include ritual sexual intercourse, either actual or in symbol. Usually, the high priestess and priest act out the Great Rite. In the northern hemisphere the Great Rite appears around May 1 at the festival of Beltane, and around November 1 in the southern hemisphere.

PART XII: DIVINATION

Wiccans rely on various forms of divination to work their craft. Astrology and numerology are two chief forms of determining the future and making decisions.

Divination is deemed useful in making day-to-day decisions. Besides the aforementioned practices, the pendulum, runes, and tarot cards are commonly used.

PART XIII: SKYCLAD

"Skyclad" means naked. Doing ritual, the coven may be Skyclad. The nine foot in diameter circle accommodates thirteen people, often six couples and a high priestess. (This arrangement may vary.) The concept is that within each person is power and energy that are necessary to work magick, and clothes inhibit the radiating outward of the power and energy. So, naked magick works best.

Wicca is greatly concerned with power. Gardner wrote,

"Witches are taught and believe that the power resides within their bodies which they can release in various ways, the simplest being dancing round in a circle, singing or shouting, to induce a frenzy; this power they believe exudes from their bodies, clothes impeding its release."[35]

The circle is also there to retain the power of the witches as opposed to the magicians or sorcerers circle which is intended to keep "evil" forces out.

Gerald Gardner was asked, "Why do you say that witches work naked?" His answer was, "I can only say: Because they do."[36] And they do so for the above reason, at least that is the general spin. If it is other than that, if these people are not aroused by naked flesh, then they are indeed on a higher plane than most normal people.

PART XIV: THE POWER AND PULL OF WICCA

However contradictory this might now seem, there are credible reasons why Wicca would be attractive. For instance, Gerald Gardner stated, "I have known many atheists who have entered the Cult and said, 'It is so lovely to find a religion in which you can believe.'"[37] Writing in the 1950s he said that Wicca (Gardner usually spelled Wicca "Wica") preserved for the Age of Aquarius reincarnation and karma, which he noted was widely embraced in the ancient world but had suffered a retreat when the Church grew in dominance.[38] He actually predicted a phenomenon that is generally understood and acknowledged, when he wrote,

> But we are today upon the threshold of a new Age. Call it the Aquarian Age, the Age of Horus, or what you will. The great, clean wind of a new Cosmic Power is blow-

35 Gardner, *Witchcraft Today*, 20.
36 Ibid., 19.
37 Gardner, *The Meaning of Witchcraft*, 242.
38 Ibid., 239.

ing upon the world from the depths of space. Already it has blown away many of the cobwebs of the past. Much prudery and false modesty, for instance, has gone by the board.[39]

Wicca did more than that; to a degree it mainlined an interest in magickal rites and soul journeying. In the twenty-first century Wicca is more than alive and well. Following are some of the ways it has made inroads into or ridden on the coattails of modern culture to attract adherents:

(1) Children of nearly every culture grow up learning stories about the fantastic and the imaginary - elves, fairies, Santa Claus figures, ghosts, the deity myths of Greece and Rome - all packaged so attractively for children. Three generations have now been immersed in the delightful world of Disney characters, thus opening their minds to all things magickal.

(2) Wicca and other neo-pagan practices allow for children to remain childlike in the imagination, at least in light of the pain and burden of living life in a chaotic world.

The hidden wonders of the ancient mysteries lure young and old alike. There are secrets, mysteries that every witch initiated into the craft is sworn to never divulge, and I have found that these do, in fact, remain secret, despite the fact that most things hidden come to light sooner or later. On the other hand, the secrets of Wicca must remain such, since their broadcast might bring negativity to its adherents.

(3) The lure for power, which is ubiquitous in humans, is a driving motivation. Magic and all the vast array of that which falls under the category of the occult, provides a mechanism into that spooky yet enticing world. Witches claim that the source of their power is unknown, although they have learned to control it and use it in such a way that none are harmed.

(4) Satan is real and he is able to perform miracles. The materialist will make a direct paradigm shift toward the spiri-

---

39 Ibid., 238.

tual when demonic tricks are played out in real time and space.

(5) Wicca is different, edgy, exciting, sexy, and cool. It is the perfect stage for acting the spiritual rebel against the dominant religions. Combining all these elements gives Wicca an allure along with a barely masked sexual element. Who can resist? There but for the grace of God. . .

(6) Satan desires that people, God's creatures made in His image, worship him. The whole point of the "Temptation in the Wilderness" (see Matthew chapter 4) was an enticement acted out by Satan to have Jesus bow down and worship him. Though our aim is not to offend Wiccans, it seems obvious that Wicca is another indirect means by Satan to redirect worshippers from God to himself. Behind the Lord, the Lady, the goddess, and the god lurks the chief demon, whether this is claimed, admitted, or even known by Wiccan proponents.

(7) Wicca is a dress-up activity, a masquerade ball, or a stimulating game. The thrill of maintaining the secrecy, if not the conspiracy, is a real draw. Secret societies at one time were the rage, and in Wicca the game is back.

(8) Wicca gives meaning to those in search of it. It is not an overstatement to say that women dominate Wicca and most other forms of witchcraft. Meaning and power go together well. Meaning attaches itself to the maxim to harm none but rather do good and especially for the "self." Power over people, events, and circumstances through magick is power nonetheless – a significant enticement.

PART XV: A QUESTION OR TWO

Proponents of Wicca commonly boast about its ancientness as compared to Christianity, for instance. The implication is that older is better. Is old really better than something newer?

I have an old car and I have a newer car. Let me tell you, the new one is better than the old one. The old Copernican model of the universe is not as reliable as newer ones. I could go on, but it is a disingenuous argument that older is better.

Wicca is indeed old, because it is based on animism, the basis for shamanism, then infused with magical concepts. But how does this give Wicca credibility?

Another question, as mentioned previously, has to do with why Wiccans love to say they do not believe in Satan. Wiccans will sometimes admit that there are evil forces about, which they of course know how to isolate and avoid. For the most part, such evil forces, energies, and beings are left unexplained.

Wiccans are not Satanists like the followers of Anton LaVey, author of the Satanic Bible, with whom I interacted during my years as a preacher in the Haight-Ashbury in the late 1960s. In my mind there are differences, although more cosmetic than actual. Just who are the helper spirits, the supposed souls of the dead, the fairies, elves, and animal spirits, really? Might they just be minions of Satan? It is not a good idea to play fast and loose with the dark sides, assuming they can be whisked away with a sleight of hand.

PART XVI: WICCA VIEWED FROM A CHRISTIAN'S PERSPECTIVE

Is Wicca real? With all its fairies, elves, gnomes, ghosts, and far more, is it a game of make believe? Do Wiccans really believe in what they are doing? Do they actually think they are talking to dead ancestors and communicating with gods and goddesses? Or is it something else or something more? Do Wiccans themselves understand what they are involved with?

The world view held by Wiccans is that energy, live energy, is everywhere, in everything, and can be manipulated by spells and rituals. If Wiccans are right, is science wrong when it sees energy not as spiritual or personal, but as something that can be empirically measured and observed?

Is there something unknown or at least unrecognized behind Wicca? Wiccans become quite upset when accused of being in league with the devil, whose existence Wiccans vehemently deny. Yet, how do they know they are not?

One issue generally ignored by Wiccans is, what is the basis of their authority? They have no sacred book, no actual central authoritative doctrine, no revelation, and no vision. What they rely on are myths, fairy tales, and ancient concepts from a wide variety of cultures. If all Wiccan deities, gods, and goddesses were added up, the final total would be quite large. Wiccan beliefs are indeed an uncritical epistemic patch-work of myths and bizarre behavior.

Is it make-believe? A child's game not discarded? A form of rebellion against the teachings of the Bible? A demonic deception? It seems that Wicca is all of these at once.

From a Christian's perspective, Wicca embraces what the Scripture condemns. In the Torah, Deuteronomy 18:10-12, is a listing of "pagan" practices that were ubiquitous in the ancient world and which the people of Israel were to reject as false:

> There shall not be found among you anyone who burns his son or his daughter as an offering, anyone who practices divination or tells fortunes or interprets omens, or a sorcerer or a charmer or a medium or a wizard or a necromancer, for whoever does these things is an abomination to the LORD.

No, Wiccans do not burn sons or daughters or anyone else as offerings to appease idols, but the rest of it must be seen as routine in their world.

A witch might say, "So what? I prefer to worship and practice my religion any way I want." And I would heartily agree. It might be prudent to examine what else is involved, however.

This is not to say that Wiccans do not really communicate with spirits, angels, gods, and goddesses. They do, but these entities/deities are not what they present themselves to be. The short and quick answer is that they are unclean or demonic spirits in disguise.

There could not be more disparate world views than Wicca

and Christianity or biblically faithful Judaism, for that matter. Wiccans pretend to value Christianity, but they actually hate it and fear it. They know that if the Bible is correct, then they have fallen into gross deception. Not only are they worshipping false gods, but they are fully engaged with and possessed by demons whose leader is Satan himself. Whatever is gained in Wicca, the unsuspected loss is far too disturbing to contemplate. This is not child's play; life and death is determined here, and not of the physical kind.

Wiccans may become trapped by the very religion they practice. It promises freedom and power, but in time it proves to give neither and turns dark. Inside Wiccans will likely be voices that shout at them to ignore the Christians. The reason for this is that Jesus Christ is the One who has power and authority over demons who masquerade themselves as gods, goddesses, spirit guides, and so on. A cosmic spiritual battle is underway here, and ultimately the real and true God will prevail. It is only a matter of time.

For those Wiccans who read this, please see it as an attempt to speak a word of reality to you, and we hope this statement will not be seen as patronizing. Please apply critical analysis to the religion to which you have committed yourself.

CHAPTER FOUR

CHARISMA: A SURPRISE INDEED!

*C*harisma is a term that turned up from time to time while we were researching shamanism, Santería, Wicca, and the trance states. This identification is troubling for those who have been involved with charismatic Christianity, like we have, and who hold to a theology that accommodates and supports, to some degree, the charismatic gifts as recorded in the Bible.[1] The authors of this book are not cessationist, but acknowledge a present operation of the gifts of grace. Our position may more accurately be described as "semi-continuationist" or even, "semi-cessationist." We view charismatic gifts as being present during times of "awakening," but much less in evidence during "normal" times.

Charisma, as referenced in various books, articles, websites, and workbooks we consulted for this research involves practices whereby persons move into "altered states of consciousness."[2] Several authors appeared to defend the practice of entering into trance states by suggesting that, if the Christians are doing it, then it must be a mainstream and therefore acceptable custom.

Charismatics/Pentecostals may not necessarily engage in practices that would be labeled charisma, but the potential is

---

1   See Romans 12 and 1 Corinthians 12.

2   ASC is a short-hand way of referring to altered states of consciousness. Other terms that have the same meaning as altered states of consciousness are trance states, ecstasy, and the passive state of mind.

there, and the line between the two is not easily determined or even noticed.

Finding that those who engage in the occult, magic, and spiritism defend such practices by pointing to "charisma" caused us to wonder if there was anything similar going on in the general Christian community.

After surveying a number of descriptions of various forms of worship and watching dozens of videos of charisma worship, our conclusion is that charismatics/Pentecostals may not necessarily engage in practices that approach entering into trance states, but the potential is there. Some charismatic/Pentecostal worship forms can, however, foster states of mind that resemble the shamanistic and Santerían rites, rituals, and celebrations. While their Christian "worship" may not purposely be aimed at attaining a trance state, the risk is there and lines are easily blurred.

THE TRANCE STATE IN SHAMANISM, SANTERÍA, AND WICCA

Our research indicated that in shamanism,[3] Santería, and Wicca the trance or ASC was normative. For instance, the shaman depends absolutely on what Michael Harner calls the Shamanic State of Consciousness of SSC. Santería includes two features that involve ASC. One has to do with divination and the other is spiritism. Both of these are dependent on trance states, wherein a deity or some other spiritual entity takes possession of the entranced one. In the Santerían bembes – the bata drumming and dancing festival ceremonies held to honor the orishas – the dancers move to the beat of the "magical" drums and become possessed by an orisha. The entranced and possessed ones then begin to function much like mediums or shamans would. In spiritism, which is indispensable to

---

3   In general, the term "charisma" did not appear in books on shamanism as it did in books on Santería and Wicca; however, the concept of the altered state and trance state is the same.

modern Santería, dead ancestors communicate with the living. This aspect of Santería is enjoying increased popularity.

In Wicca, the trance state is crucial. Wiccans speak of the journey, sometimes called the "trance-portation," where the subject or journeyer contacts various spiritual entities. The ASC is the gateway into the journey. Most books on Wicca will provide the reader with numerous techniques calculated to move a person into a trance. The traditional pattern involves breathing, balancing, centering, grounding, followed perhaps by meditation or concentration on something or on nothing. Usually, the journeyer focuses on an object, such as a candle or an image of a deity, and this may all be accompanied by listening to music specially designed for the purpose – soothing, mellow, and nature-oriented melodies. Once in the ASC, the journeyer meets various entities that help during the soul journey, including animal familiars, spirit guides, angels, goddesses and gods, and souls of the deceased.

The trance state is an obvious connection between shamanism, Santería, and Wicca. The next question is, what about charisma? Is there a connection here as well?

MOVING TO THE BEAT

During the 1970s, while pastoring a fairly large charismatic church, I strummed my guitar and sang as part of our praise band. Essentially, I helped lead the congregation in praise and worship. For nearly a decade I did this every Sunday morning. The lyrics of the choruses we sang were typically biblically oriented, and we sang the chorus several times before moving on to the next one. Usually, the entire "worship" time lasted at most half an hour. Sometimes people stood up, swayed, and lifted their hands, but those times were fairly tame compared to what has now arrived.

Nowadays the "praise band" is ubiquitous among Pentecostal/charismatics and many Evangelicals. Yes, the name of Jesus is heard, but the music tends to drone on and on, the drumming is loud and powerful, the power point presentation contains images depicting the beauty of the earth, and a "praise chorus" can last quite a long time.[4] The lighting is sometimes manipulated, and the congregants seem lost in their swaying to the beat with arms raised and eyes closed. It sounds good and feels good, but is there something slightly wrong here?

In these venues, the music is the praise segment of the service and is often considered the worship time – the time when it is thought that God's Holy Spirit shows up. And obviously, this is the time when the beat of the drum dominates. If examined from a biblical perspective, such worship should be seen as inadequate. The early church, as revealed especially in the book of Acts in the Bible, gathered because of a shared faith in Jesus, and the Holy Spirit was present during the entirety of the time of gathering and not merely at a time when feelings and emotions were aroused by music. The early Christians considered that when two or three gathered together, God was present – God the Father, God the Son, and God the Holy Spirit (see Matthew 18:20).

People who routinely experience such modern lost-in-the-music worship most often say it is their favorite part of the service.[5] This is when their burden is lifted and they feel connected to God. Here, they feel, is where they *experience* God. And therein lies the difficulty: it is feeling-oriented. Those who were or are still old time rock-and-rollers now experience in their worship much the same sensations and feelings that were generated while listening to the rock bands; attending worship is akin to being at a rock concert, complete with the

---

4   Some of us refer to worship being the "Seven - Eleven" time: songs with seven words sung eleven times.

5   One objection sometimes voiced is, "Why should the Devil get all the good music?" Enjoying good music is not the issue here; rather it is the state of mind to which the music can lead. The Lord our God has all the best music, and the goodness of it is not dependent on the beat but upon the meaning of the words, phrases, and stanzas sung.

need for earplugs. Many people report that they are lost in the presence of God. Some of these people also recount that, in these moments, they sometimes speak to angels or saints and are even transported to the "third heaven"[6] to converse with Jesus Himself.

Is it possible that worshippers move into a trance state without realizing it? If they do recognize themselves as being in a different state of mind, do they simply assume it is all of God? A broader and more serious question is, could demonic forces produce such a dramatic deception?

CONTEMPLATIVE PRAYER[7]

For three or more decades there has been a renewed interest in mysticism among Christians. Retreats for clergy often emphasize "contemplative prayer," and the spiritual disciplines of those considered saints, such as Teresa of Avila, John of the Cross, and Ignatius Loyola, are discussed and practiced. It is obvious that these veered sharply away from biblical models of prayer. The style of meditation these "saints" practiced does not match what is mentioned in biblical passages, which stress a focused, mindful, thinking of who God is and what He has done. Much if not most of the current revival of contemplative praying should not be mistaken for the biblical practice.

Jesus taught His followers how to pray; He even provided a model prayer – the Lord's Prayer – and this prayer was a deliberate and conscious voicing of concerns and praise to God. In every case where prayer is described in the New Testament, nothing approaches instructions to settle, center, breathe, visualize, concentrate, blank out the mind, or focus on anything in particular.

---

6   See Section 2-4 "Biblical Considerations" for the fullest explanation of "third heaven."

7   Contemplative prayer will be further examined in the next chapter.

SOAKING PRAYER

Beyond contemplative prayer is "soaking prayer." What is called soaking prayer has been around since the beginning of the twenty-first century, yet it is neither widely known nor understood. One's first assumption might be that it involves long periods of time spent in prayer to God. However, what it really involves is something quite different.

Soaking prayer is in reality a mystical activity. Since it is often described as "resting in God's presence," it appears to be innocuous and biblical. This is how many are drawn into it, especially when charismatic church leaders embrace it.

Proponents of soaking prayer are convinced it is nothing more than "positioning yourself to express your love to God." To get to that stage, however, some quiet instrumental or worship music must pervade the environment, while the participants often lie on the floor. The mind eventually settles down and focuses on God, or so it is thought. The attitude of the participant is to be, "God, do what you want to in me." After some period, perhaps hours, there might be laughter, crying, or shaking – all supposedly coming from the Holy Spirit. The goal of soaking prayer or a possible end point of it is that the Holy Spirit would give the person a vision or bring a memory to mind that needs healing.

Another emphasis of soaking prayer is that it brings a person into a state of deep rest. Soaking prayer almost always is accompanied by the playing of gentle worship songs, with the participants sitting or lying down. It may involve the repeated praying of short prayers for an extended period of time. It is reminiscent of a devotee of Hinduism chanting a mantra.

Persons practicing soaking prayer attempt to keep their minds free of thoughts and concerns. They continue this until they feel a sensation in the body, perhaps a tingling of the skin, a perception of heat or cold, or a breeze gently blowing upon the body. When this happens, the desired stage has been reached, and one experiences being in the presence of God. The soaking praying may begin innocently enough, but after a while, the participants are in a meditative state of mind. It is here that any connection to biblical prayer has been abandoned.

The following explanation of soaking prayer was found online under the heading "Embark on an intimate journey": "The Secret Place is not just a listening experience. It is a journey of soaking worship. It is a place of intimacy with the Father, a place where the heart longs for His touch." In that same website, where music for soaking prayer may be obtained, a soaking prayer facilitator's comment addressed to a composer of music used for soaking prayer reads:

> I prepare the sanctuary to become a resting place for the Lord as people come to soak in His presence. The lights are turned down, there are candles, and the atmosphere is that of intimacy. For three hours we seek His face together and listen to your music, which invites His presence to come. I lead it at our Soaking Prayer Centre at the church and many of our soakers really like it. It is anointed and I have had some awesome visions of angels and God's glory while worshipping with it in the background.[8]

It is disappointing how similar this sounds to Wiccan techniques used to enter a trance state. And there appears to be an addictive quality to soaking prayer; people crave it and think other forms of worship are boring and devoid of God's Spirit.

SOZO PRAYER

The next step out on our continuum is "sozo prayer," or "sozo ministry." Sozo comes from the Greek word for save or deliver. The goal of sozo is laudable, and that is to get to the root of those things that prevent a Christian from entering into a deeper personal relationship with God.

---

8   Found at http://www.secretplaceministries.org

Sozo is very mystical in its approach and departs dramatically from any biblical precedent. Those engaged in sozo prayer are encouraged by a mediator/guide to enter into a mild trance state. The mediator/guide then leads a person "into a series of mental/emotional rooms or stages, where, by connecting to their own deep feelings and thoughts, they believe themselves to have a new experience with God."[9]

Where soaking prayer is found, sozo will be close by as well. The motive is to "experience God," and it is difficult to make a case against that desire. However, we have no scriptural mandate to experience God through our emotions or feelings; it is instead a matter of faith. The Bible does not actually teach that we are to *experience* God; we are to trust in and believe in God. I have found no place in the New Testament where anyone, including Jesus, Peter, John, or Paul, instructs believers to "experience God." While we may sense that God is present with us, that is a different focus of our attention. Under discussion here is the seeking after sensations or feelings. Christians must be clear; our faith is not feeling-centered. We must not equate human feelings with the Spirit.

IS THERE BIBLICAL PRECEDENT OR WARRANT FOR SOAKING PRAYER AND SOZO PRAYER?

Biblically oriented Christians desire to pursue knowledge of God through what He has revealed in Scripture, Old and New Testaments, rather than to seek a subjective, experience-driven union with God. And this is because there are counterfeit, demonically powered mechanisms depending on that attitude, which promise incredible spiritual breakthroughs, but which ultimately cannot deliver them.

A way of testing the spirits to determine whether they are from God (see 1 John 4) is to ask whether the spiritual process

9   From the website, *Got Questions*, specifically www.gotquestions.org/sozo-prayer.html.

that brought them has clearly defined *biblical precedents*, and lacking clarity there, to see whether there is *biblical warrant* for the doctrine, theology, or practice supporting it.

Can *biblical precedent* be found that indicates well-defined evidence in the Scripture to support the prayer processes discussed here under the rubric of soaking, sozo, or contemplative prayer?

A short statement is sufficient: there is no such evidence. Some might make reference to certain things in the life of a number of persons spoken of in the Bible for support of so-called Christian style passive states of mind. Clearly, however, Jesus' teachings on prayer assume mindful and thoughtful petitions to the Father who is in heaven. There is nothing in the writings of Paul, John, Peter, James, or Jude that approach what is advocated in the forms of prayer under consideration.[10]

Is *biblical warrant* set by one or more statements in Scripture that might lend themselves to be in support of the forms of prayer in question? Again the answer is the same: there is none. Obscure verses from the Psalms, taken out of context, will not do. Neither Jesus nor any New Testament author referred to or used passages from the Old Testament to justify questionable forms of prayer. All of them knew prayer to be the expressing of mind and heart to God the Father who hears prayer.

With neither precedent nor warrant, some still attempt to label such practices as Christian and urge others into strange mechanisms to achieve an experience with God. These forms are not Christian but are normative in religions based upon shamanistic underpinnings, such as Santería, Wicca, Hinduism, some forms of Buddhism (especially Tibetan Buddhism), and other spiritual practices focused on deep meditation or concentration techniques.

More worrisome is the fact that these methods are dan-

---

10 See the chapter "Biblical Considerations" for more on this topic.

gerous. Most Wiccans believe that the entities they encounter in their journeys are not simply a product of the imagination but are real *benign beings*. They have no proof of their benevolence, however, and my work, experience, and research says otherwise. The gods, goddesses, guides, helpers, elves, fairies, animal spirits, dead ancestors, and so on, have a common denominator: they are actually demons in disguise. Unhappily, I must use the same description of events for those entering into trance-like states through soaking, sozo, and contemplative prayer and meditation.

However easy it might be to defend and protect or to argue and justify, a better strategy is a critical examination of the practices to which one has committed, because the consequences of living in error must not be taken lightly.

CHRISTIAN SHAMANISM?

Kat Kerr is the latest in a stream of Christians or persons of religion who present themselves as what is known in other contexts as psychics or mediums.

In her book, *Revealing Heaven: An Eyewitness Account*, she claims she has been caught up to heaven and while there has talked face-to-face with the "Father." During her frequent visits to heaven, she converses with the dead and brings back messages of their well being to loved ones on earth. Here is a typical shaman, cloaked in Christian orthodoxy, who travels out of the body, supposedly to heaven.

By means of a series of YouTube videos she brings regular "Revelation Reports." She claims heaven exists inside the created universe and is thus material. Her descriptions include guardian angels, warehouses from which angels will one day bring human body parts to earth and heal many people, God's secret agents doing special miraculous feats by which they earn themselves large mansions in heaven, "stop stations" where God's guardian angels visit and inhabit and where miracles occur – and much, much more. This is all enthusiastically accepted by many Christians, particularly those who identify with Pentecostalism.

Interestingly, throughout her videos, Kerr presents much that is theologically normative. It is some truth mixed with much error, which makes it difficult to find fault. After studying her videos, I am fairly convinced that she is no charlatan or trickster. She comes across as a real Christian; she is passionate; she says all the right things for the average charismatic or pentecostal-oriented person, especially the younger set; she quotes Scripture, loves Jesus, and so on. Yet the connection with shamanism is unmistakable. It seems that the "age-old religion" has made inroads not just into Santería and Wicca, but also into certain segments of the broad Christian community.

THE "FIRE" CONTROVERSY

Before concluding this chapter, the current debate or controversy between the "continuationist" camp and the "cessationist" camp deserves comment, since it is a controversy about the gifts of the Holy Spirit that is powerfully engaging a significant segment of the Christian community.

John MacArthur, pastor of Grace Community Church in Sun Valley, California (a church I have attended over the years while visiting my home town Sunland-Tujunga), is the author of many fine works. His book entitled *Strange Fire* was published by Nelson Books in 2013. He is also a major force behind the "Strange Fire Conferences," videos of which are readily available for viewing on the internet. Pastor MacArthur, whom I highly regard and respect, holds a cessationist point of view that considers the charismatic gifts of the Holy Spirit listed in Romans 12 and 1 Corinthians 12 as no longer operative in the Church today.

Michael L. Brown has written a rebuttal to MacArthur's book entitled *Authentic Fire*, published by Excel Publishers in 2014. He argues for the continuationist point of view that the charismatic gifts of the Holy Spirit, as listed in Romans 12 and 1 Corinthians 12, are yet operative in the Church today. My wife, Katie Philpott, a Jewish believer in Jesus, as is Michael Brown, has for years enjoyed and profited from his work, especially his apologetics series, *Answering Jewish Objections to Jesus*, published by BakerBooks.

We travel a somewhat different road than either of these respected Christian leaders. After agonizing over the issues presented by both men, we find ourselves, as noted in the first paragraph of this chapter, straddling the theological fence. It is not a case of being unable to make up our minds or desiring to somehow distance ourselves from the controversy; rather it is that our semi-cessationist or semi-continuationist view, which is not considered by either MacArthur or Brown, is closer to how we see things biblically.

This view is simply that the charismatic gifts do continue in the Church but are rarely seen in "normal" times like they might be seen in "awakening" times.

If we had to choose sides we would declare with Pastor MacArthur. Twice in his book Brown mentions "trance" and acknowledges that charismatic/Pentecostals will experience these states of consciousness and that they are acceptable. This is problematic, because the same is found in the shamanistic religions examined in this book. In fact, the trance state is the door opener to the soul journey and essential for these demonic and pagan religious practices. The growing presence of trance states experienced in charismatic/Pentecostal worship, especially as produced by certain forms of music, is too dangerous to ignore.

A warning against infusing Christian practice with the trance state has thus far been ignored by the charismatic/ Pentecostal communities, perhaps because those who enter the trance states and begin prophesying in these venues are admired and achieve a higher status than those who do not, just as in shamanism, Santería, and Wicca. This trend is nearly out of control in the Pentecostal settings of some third world countries, especially in Africa.

Those who enter trance states, no matter where, how, and why, expose themselves to demonic spirits and will eventually need to face the reality of their spiritual condition and seek deliverance from demonic oppression.

PROPHECY – A SOURCE OF CONFUSION

One last point: The concepts of prophet and prophecy are key sources for causing confusion. Both MacArthur and Brown accept a similar point of view when it comes to prophecy (one against and the other for) and view it as a *fore*telling rather than a *forth*telling. Our view is that the prophet declares, proclaims, or preaches the Word of God as revealed in the Scripture from Genesis to Revelation. Nothing new or additional needs to be revealed. The command of Jesus is clear: we are to be witnesses of the gospel of Jesus Christ, and this witness, in our view, directs the work of prophets.[11]

THE WARNING – NOT MADE LIGHTLY

We do not relish the possibility of being seen as discouragers of people, causing them to question their view of God. While it is more enjoyable to encourage and applaud efforts to establish a deeper relationship with the Maker of heaven and earth, I must come back to the reality that if it can be reasonably discerned that someone will run into danger just beyond the curve in the road, it is negligence not to raise the alarm and call out for caution.

Tolerance and diversity are two concepts that are much applauded and honored, and to a degree, rightfully so. Blind acceptance, however, can be dangerously negligent. Fearing to

---

11 For a fuller treatment of this view, go to www.earthenvesseljournal.com and search in the Site Map for Kent's essay entitled, "The Prophet, the Preacher."

offend or be seen as out of step with contemporary cultural ideals may result in allowing error to go unchallenged. This we cannot do.

At the heart of this book is a warning against the mental, emotional, and spiritual danger that lurks in the trance state, which is the gateway to the "soul journey," which is the means of introducing the soul journeyer to the world of demons. Wherever it might be encountered, in shamanism, Santería, Wicca, the occult, or unbiblical Christian forms of prayer or worship, the trance state is the connection between them.

Christians have always stood against unbiblical theologies, doctrines, and methodologies. The examples of this are abundant in Scripture, with Old Testament prophets like Isaiah and Jeremiah, and in the New Testament with Jesus and Paul, but also in the biblical books written by John, James, Jude, and Peter. They did not do so out of spite or ill will, but out of a concern to point out the dangers of counterfeit spiritualities and practices.

CHAPTER FIVE

CHRISTIAN MYSTICISM

W hat is broadly known as Christian mysticism has existed for many centuries. The mystics' quest was for "more" of God, to experience Him directly and personally. Within Christian mysticism is contemplative prayer, which is distinct from either vocal recitation of words, mental reflection, or mental meditation on God's word and its meaning and application.

Kat Kerr's journeys into heaven to speak with the Father, as discussed in the Charisma chapter, also fit into the classification of Christian mysticism. Within this chapter are other examples of mysticism, not all of which are or claim to be Christian in orientation: the work of Richard Foster, Mirabai Starr, Richard Rohr, and Sarah Young.

A CONNECTION WITH CHRISTIANITY

Contemplative prayer shares a broad theology common to mainstream and historic Christianity. It may, however, involve certain techniques that result in a state of mind resembling or identical to an altered state of consciousness or ecstasy, which then moves it into a category similar to shamanism, Santería, Wicca, and charisma.

While a doctoral student at San Francisco Theological Seminary in San Anselmo, California, (Presbyterian), I learned about contemplative forms of Christianity. At first I was attracted to these and read somewhat extensively in the area, even attending retreats where contemplative prayer was practiced. For some reason it never worked with me; in fact, I would engage in rather heated debates with some of the "spiritual mentors" or "spiritual directors" enlisted there. In any case, I learned firsthand what was involved.[1]

I want to be clear that there is much in what is called contemplative prayer that I value and actually cherish. We are called to love God with all of our being, and the truth is, in our human weakness, we rarely experience a very deep love for God and what He has done for us in Christ. There are times when I long for nothing more than to simply be alone with my Bible, read favorite passages, settle back and think of Him, and pray and talk and reflect. This is normative and healthy. What I am addressing in this chapter is quite different, something that crosses the line, however faint, into an altered state of consciousness. It is that state, often called ecstasy, especially in shamanism, that exposes a person to invasion by entities that are indeed spiritual but not holy.

RICHARD J. FOSTER

Richard J. Foster is often associated with contemplative prayer. His book, *Celebration of Discipline*, published in 1978 by Harper & Row, dramatically impacted many in the years after its first appearance and is still widely used in Bible colleges and seminaries around the world. In the year following its publication, it was our primary text for a class called Spiritual Formation, which was part of my doctoral curriculum. Foster divides his twelve disciplines into three categories: Inward, Outward, and Corporate. In the first category, the Inward Dis-

---

1   Despite rejecting certain features of the contemplative prayer learned in the 1970s, I still value meditation centered on God and His Word. Since that time I have prepared Gospel Meditations based on specific passages of Scripture and published them in the weekly bulletin for Sunday worship. A collection of these is under construction for those interested in meditative spirituality void of mystically-oriented forms.

ciplines are meditation, prayer, fasting, and study.[2] Though I
still deem much of the material in the book to fit within a broad
Christian and biblical range, I consider that the very first of the
Inward Disciplines, "Meditation," crosses the aforementioned
faint line. Let me explain.

Foster indicates his awareness that Eastern forms of meditation involve the attempt to empty the mind. Then he says,
"Christian meditation is an attempt to empty the mind in order
to fill it."[3] It *sounds* good, but is emptying the mind normative
for the Christian? In my opinion, it crosses the line and has neither biblical precedent nor warrant.[4] Christians should indeed
desire the "mind of Christ" (1 Corinthians 2:16b) but that does
not suggest an emptying of the mind but a transforming "by
the renewal of the mind" (Romans 12:2).

Foster also speaks of the Eastern meditative process of
detachment, especially as it relates to Buddhism. He acknowledges that detachment from the confusion of the world around
us is not the goal for Christians but that Christians actually go
beyond that. He implies that the Christian must go through
detachment to reach *attachment*. Again the difficulty is that
many would simply say amen to this without questioning the
idea of the Christian *need* to detach. To me, this is the perfect
set up for a significant deviation from healthy and scriptural
prayer and meditation.

Even more problematic is what he says later: "It is wonder-

---

2   I was much taken by Foster's work and attempted to explore it to
the extent possible and to seriously engage myself in each of the twelve
disciplines. I *lived* with the book for many months.

3   Richard J. Foster, *Celebration of Discipline*, 15.

4   By "precedent and warrant" I mean that, for a Christian to engage
in such processes, it should be clearly evident that Jesus engaged in such
meditation with His disciples, that such is found in the life of the primitive
Church and thus recorded in the Book of Acts, and that such practice is
mentioned in apostolic New Testament letters. But there is no such evidence and therefore no biblical precedent or warrant for such a practice.

ful when a particular meditation leads to ecstasy. . .."[5] When I first encountered this I was much impressed, but after some attempts at what I thought was "ecstasy," I gave up and fortunately so. The desire for ecstasy might have led me deeper into an Eastern style of meditation, to the point of going into an altered state of consciousness and thus exposing myself to invasion by unwanted and unclean spirits.

It is precisely for this reason that the influence of Foster finally aroused my critique. What might seem harmless and even appear to conform to some of the experiences of well known Christian mystics like John of the Cross, Teresa of Avila, and others, is in fact extremely dangerous and little different from where shamanism, Santería, and Wicca take their practitioners.

It gets worse. Here are two sentences from Foster's book that even more closely resemble the teachings of the religions named above: "All who acknowledge Jesus Christ as Lord are the universal priesthood of God and as such can enter the Holy of Holies and converse with the living God. It seems so difficult to bring people to believe that they can hear God's voice."[6]

On the one hand Foster expresses the biblical truth that in Christ we are seated with Him in the heavenly places, but he reaches too far in his declaration that we actually ought to hear the voice of God. Granted, there were those biblical incidents where it is reported that people heard the voice of God. These were the prophets and others, like Peter at Joppa in the run-up to the conversion of the Roman Centurion Cornelius, but it is not something found elsewhere in the Bible as a normal and regular spiritual practice. Conversations with various spirit entities are common, however, among shamans, Santerían priests and priestesses, and among witches of neo-pagan religions. This must give one pause.

It gets even worse with Foster. Still in the chapter on med-

5 Ibid., 17.
6 Ibid., 19.

itation, he speaks of dreams. He teaches that a Christian can invite God to inform us through our dreams. "We should tell Him of our willingness to allow Him to speak to us in this way. ... We simply ask God to surround us with the light of His protection as he ministers to our spirit."[7] This is characteristic of Wiccan teaching, not biblical teaching. Nowhere in Scripture is there anything approaching this. It is mediumistic and spiritistic – the province of the occult.

Foster goes on to say, "After awhile there is a deep yearning within to go into the upper regions beyond the clouds. In your imagination allow your spiritual body, shining with light, to rise out of your physical body. Go deeper and deeper into outer space until there is nothing except the warm presence of the eternal Creator. Rest in His presence. Listen quietly, anticipating the unanticipated. Note carefully any instruction given."[8] Here Foster seems to promote, regardless of whether only "in the imagination," out-of-body travel, also called astral projection, definitely belonging to the province of the shaman.

These concepts are reminiscent of some of the errors found in charisma, in which more and more is asked, even demanded, of God. In charisma, people recently report to be conversing with angels and even Jesus. An acquaintance who is a proponent of having conversations with deity said, "You do not have to read the Scripture anymore, you can go direct." This connects with shamanism generally, and especially with Santería and Wicca, in my view.

BEYOND FOSTER

In the years from 1980 onward, I heard little of contemplative spirituality, and when I did it was from books by those who identified with the Emerging Church Movement, but not always. Though not a large emphasis among Christians, the

7   Ibid., 23.
8   Ibid., 27.

quest for "more," a deeper spirituality, was evident. Contemplative prayer is closely connected with meditation, but it is not the kind of meditation we find in the Bible, which is focused, alert, and thoughtful attention on God, who He is, and what He has done in His Son, Jesus Christ. In sharp contrast, contemplative prayer encourages an emptying of the mind in order to achieve a light, moderate, or deep altered state of consciousness.

To do contemplative or centering prayer, one technique is to focus on a word and repeat that word over and over, much like a Buddhist mantra. The word chosen should have spiritual significance or meaning to the one praying. Perhaps one concentrates on a single lit candle or speaks a series of prayers, but the intent is to open one's mind, soul, and heart to God. Contemplative prayer deliberately encourages the pursuit of a mystical experience with God, and the emphasis is on "experience."

MIRABAI STARR: A CONNECTION WITH CONTEMPORARY MYSTICISM

The autumn 2012 issue of *Light of Consciousness: a Journal of Spiritual Awakening* contains an article by Mirabai Starr entitled, "Contemplative Life."[9] Starr points out that many of the world's religions, including Christianity, have contemplative states. Contemplation, meditation, interior prayer, mental prayer, and centering prayer are essentially synonymous terms and describe means of meeting with the "Divine Presence" that Starr writes about. I agree with her. It is in such states of consciousness that a person will encounter *otherness*, the place considered to be where the Divine Presence reveals itself.

Starr then describes a process whereby, in my view, a person becomes invaded by the "divine" presences (earlier, we

---

9   Mirabai Starr is one of the best known and respected teachers and authors of meditation and contemplation today. She has a deep interest in Hinduism, Sufism, Judaism, and mystical Christian practices.

called them by various terms, including spirit guides, etc.) that show up in the altered state. She outlines three stages of the process: Stage one is termed purgation or *via purgativa*. This is where a person surrenders and leaves behind whatever god conceptions he or she has. So, the door swings open to whatever is waiting to come in.

Stage two is *via illuminativa*, where that which is divine, the divine light, is poured into the now purged, clean, and waiting empty vessel. During this stage the captivation of the one praying or meditating takes place. In my view, this is where possession by unclean spirits occurs.

Stage three is union, or *via unitiva*. This is similar to the union sought for in Yoga and is the real and actual intent or purpose of Yoga.[10] Here the self, or what little is left of it, joins with or merges with the One[11] and actually disappears. Starr points out that this is precisely what the Christian mystics were aiming at in their contemplative practices – to be at one with God, to be in union with the Almighty. But, with what were John of the Cross and Teresa of Avila really in touch? What they were engaged in, and what Mirabai Starr recognizes in them and advocates, is nothing close to biblical or historic Christianity.[12]

One of the chief points Starr makes is that the deep meditative state will change a person dramatically due to the profound spiritual insights thereby attained. I agree with her. As

---

10   Yoga means union, with the All, the Universe, the One Supreme Being, and so on. Yoga, as only exercise, is Yoga in name only and is usually practiced in the West as nothing more than exercise.

11   The "One" can be variously interpreted or understood depending on the religious concepts held by the one meditating.

12   We humans are basically repelled by holiness, and in a bizarre, even perverse way are attracted to the unholy. Prior to my conversion at age twenty-one, I shied away from Christians, because they seemed to be "holier than thou." My friends and I embraced darker alternatives that seemed to be more fun. What Starr advocates looks and is spiritual but is not holy. For those who have not been touched by the grace of God in Christ, Starr's pagan spirituality is oddly attractive.

mentioned before, when one encounters genuine spirituality, actual and real spirit, one is transformed. That person will immediately abandon strict materialism and gravitate toward the spiritual and the mystical, almost regardless of what religion or spiritual practice is the attraction – Christianity, Hinduism, Buddhism, Sufism, Santería, Wicca, Charisma, or other. This meets my own experience in four decades of work as a pastor of Christian churches. Once again, it is necessary to recognize that much that is spiritual is neither good nor God.

Satan is the master of deceit; if he is thought of as only evil and demonic, then deception is all the more probable. The demonic kingdom with which we are faced, including "the rulers, the authorities, the cosmic powers, the spiritual forces of evil in the heavenly places" (see Ephesians 6:12), will appear grand beyond description. In fact, Satan can have an appearance so attractive, he is referred to as Lucifer, the "angel of light" (see 2 Corinthians 11:14). With such power and confidence that he targeted Jesus Himself, would we not be targets?

RICHARD ROHR AND "FALLING UPWARD: A SPIRITUALITY FOR THE TWO HALVES OF LIFE"[13]

For many people, the tragedies, traumas, failures, and disappointments common to the first half of life can be a catalyst for change, according to Richard Rohr. Once the idealistic views of life fall away, a person may recognize that there must be more, and this more involves the pursuit of God. His analogy is that rather than falling down when trouble descends, one may fall upward.

In his book, *Falling Upward: A Spirituality for the Two Halves of Life*, Father Richard Rohr, a Franciscan priest, speaks to the reality of living in a fallen world and being fallen peo-

---

13 *Falling Upward* was published in 2011 by Jossey-Bass, A Wiley Imprint. I was given the book by a friend who had been given a copy of it by a pastor of a large seeker friendly church in Los Angeles. This pastor recommended the book for growth in Christian maturity and spirituality.

ple. It is the nature of the "path" for falling upward rather than downward that I want to address.

Clues to the actual nature of the "path" are apparent in the blurbs on the back of the dust cover. They are as follows: Joanna Macy, author of *World as Lover, World as Self*, writes, "*Falling Upward* calls forth the promise within us and frees us to follow it into wider dimensions of our spiritual authenticity."

Brian McLaren, author of *A New Kind of Christianity* and *Naked Spirituality* writes, "Richard offers a simple but deeply helpful framework for seeing the whole spiritual life – one that will help both beginners on the path as they look ahead and long-term pilgrims as they look back over their journey so far."[14]

Jim Finley, Merton scholar and author of *The Contemplative Heart*, writes, "We begin to see that, as we grow older, we are being awakened to deep, simple, and mysterious things we simply could not see when we were younger."

Finally, from Cynthia Bourgeault, Episcopal priest and author of *The Meaning of Mary Magdalene, Centering Prayer, Inner Awakening*, and *The Wisdom of Knowing* comes, "This is Richard Rohr at his vintage best: prophetic, pastoral, practical. A book I will gratefully share with my children and grandchildren." While each of these endorsements is vague, the implication here is mind expansion of the variety considered in this book.

Rohr states that his favorite mystic is Lady Julian of Norwich, who lived from 1342 to 1416.[15] After falling deathly ill, she received sixteen mystical revelations, usually entitled, "Revelations of Divine Love." She is venerated in the Anglican and Lutheran churches but was not made a saint in the Catholic Church. In her visions she saw God as loving, not wrathful,

---

14 Brian McLaren is identified as an evangelical Christian and as a leader within the Emerging Church movement.

15 From Rohr's Introduction, xx.

that all people would experience His love and have salvation (she is referred to by some as a "proto-universalist"), and most importantly, that sin is necessary to enable people to begin to discover the higher way of love. It is easy to see why Richard Rohr would embrace her.

The Christian mystics, Saints Teresa of Avila, Ignatius of Loyola, John of the Cross, and even Francis of Assisi, among many other less known Christians, focused on turning inward by means of deep prayer, meditation, and contemplation.

Characteristic of their experiences in such mind states were visions, revelations, and words of prophecy. These were problematic, because they often contained theology that differed, and sometimes markedly so, with Scripture. But the revelations were accepted by some as coming from divine and therefore holy sources and not to be easily dismissed. The appeal of the ancient mystics is currently undergoing yet another renaissance.

Rohr's concepts are an excellent example of importing concepts from mystical, even occult oriented, religions into spiritual practices for Christians. The popularity of this process is partially due to the fact that there are spiritual or mystical experiences connected with such practices that are entirely convincing and captivating.

In the back of Rohr's book is a list of related resources and recordings that are published by the Center for Action and Contemplation. The following quote is revealing:

In January 2008, James Finley and Fr. Richard Rohr gave a conference in Albuquerque, sharing The Four Noble Truths of the Buddha, the distilled essence of Buddhist teaching. In these talks, each Truth was introduced and explored, with emphasis given to the presence of these truths at the heart of Jesus' call to awaken to God's presence in every detail of our lives.

SARAH YOUNG AND "JESUS CALLING": WHO IS ACTUALLY ON THE OTHER END?[16]

"Rest in My Presence, allowing Me to take charge of this day. Do not bolt into the day like a racehorse suddenly released. Instead, walk purposefully with Me, letting Me direct your course one step at a time." "You are on the right path. Listen more to Me, and less to your doubts. I am leading you along the way designed just for you." "As you focus your thoughts on Me, be aware that I am fully attentive to you." "You must discipline yourself to live within the boundaries of today. It is in the present moment that I walk close to you, helping you carry your burdens." "Come to Me with a teachable spirit, eager to be changed."

The above are but a few of the hundreds of affirming statements Sarah says Jesus spoke to her over the years. It is no wonder her books, principally *Jesus Calling* (published by Thomas Nelson), have become bestsellers. People who buy her books also read Joel Osteen, Joyce Meyer, and others in the health, wealth, and prosperity genre.

Young is referred to as a woman of listening prayer. She prays then waits for Jesus to answer. She strongly affirms that He does, yet she says she does not hear an audible voice. She listens then writes or journals what Jesus places on her heart. But at the same time, she claims that what she hears in her heart are the actual words of Jesus. Inexplicably, however, she depends on the Holy Spirit to determine if what she hears from Jesus is biblically correct! This is more than just slightly confused and confusing.

Young wanted "more," and she wanted it now, on this side of heaven. She knew the Bible was the word of God but she yearned for more. The indwelling of the Holy Spirit was not

---

16 Sarah Young and Jesus Calling are discussed in the previous chapter, but her work falls more into the realm of contemplative prayer than charisma.

enough; the Scripture alone did not satisfy; she wanted and needed more. I have noticed that when people want more they will get more, and if they want to hear from God directly they will, sooner or later, hear someone or something speaking.

Most, if not all, of the "words of Jesus" spoken to Young are directed to her personally. She is instructed to do this and that – trust, know, believe, and so on, all expressed in the first person, "Me," meaning Jesus. Her devotional books are purported to be a recitation of what Jesus said to her.

It is difficult to determine if some sort of altered state of consciousness is involved in Young's praying, but I suspect it is. I have known a number of parishioners who became so totally immersed in deep prayer they would lose track of time and place. I have experienced this myself. This was during a time when I was practicing the techniques taught by Richard Foster in his *Celebration of Discipline*. Being alone, quieting myself, breathing deeply, tuning out distractions, suppressing worldly concerns, sitting in a beautiful and peaceful place, perhaps with soothing music playing in the background – I could feel myself slipping into a light trance. And when I felt this happen I would become frightened to some degree and pull away. My personal experience informs me of how dangerous it is to put oneself in a spiritually exposed position, straining to listen in order to hear what God might say.

Young's Jesus is rather limited in what He says to her. There are continual streams of, "You are on the right path," "Relax and trust in Me," "I am with you," and "Listen to Me." These words of Jesus are rather imbalanced, however. His messages are encouraging and never otherwise; the pithy little sayings are decidedly skewed to the positive. But Jesus in Scripture is far different from this. A quick perusal in the Gospels of Matthew, Mark, Luke, and John will make it clear that Sarah's Jesus is not the Jesus of the Bible.

There is no actual Gospel message in what Jesus supposedly says to Sarah Young. This ought to make one suspicious.

Not that what Sarah hears is unbiblical, but the whole of it is sub-Christian at best.

At worst (and there *is* a worst) is that Young is listening to something or someone who is not Jesus at all but is rather *imitating* and *counterfeiting* Jesus. Helen Schuchman listened to the voice of what she thought was Jesus and came up with the Course in Miracles, a clearly mediumistic deception. Is Young following in her footsteps? My view is, yes!

But the concerns do not stop there. Beyond Young's descriptions of what she has experienced is her suggestion that others may also hear Jesus calling. Sarah's books have therefore become for some a school for mediums. Naiveté on the reader's part coupled with intent to deceive on the part of whoever or whatever is speaking to Young is an extremely dangerous combination.

Sarah Young's listening prayer presents a slightly different scenario from much of Christian mysticism. She does not seem to obviously seek an altered state of consciousness. However, it is in the listening mode where a light trance state may be entered, even without attempting to do so. Christian, biblically-oriented praying does not involve listening for an audible reply. In that restful, contemplative state, the listening for an actual "still small voice" is the locus of concern, especially for those who have practiced going into deep meditative states of mind. The most powerful shamans can move easily into and out of their ecstasy, so that, over time, an altered state may envelope the one praying without intentionality. Again, when one is in such a state and hears a voice, the question must be asked, who is the speaker?

Summing Up

Contemplative prayer, shamanism, Santería, Wicca, and charisma all have a common denominator, a connection that is the passive or altered state of consciousness, regardless of the means of getting there. While in such states of mind, encountering spirits seldom seems horrific and demonic. Rather, these beings seem benign, majestic, angelic, powerful, awesome, even holy, and therein is their captivating nature. These religious spiritualities bring their practitioners into the realm of beings, entities, and spirits, but they are unclean and demonic deceivers. This, I realize, is virtually impossible to accept for one captivated by spiritual forces.

The dots are once more connected: the practices encouraged in books like Rohr's and Young's lead to the trance state, whether light, moderate, or deep. These states of consciousness, common to forms of Buddhism (especially Tibetan), Hinduism, Islam's Sufism, Judaism's Kabbalah, shamanism, Santería, Wicca (and other neo-pagan religious expressions), and charisma open the door to spiritual beings that can be enlightening and powerful but not holy.

CHAPTER SIX

THE SOUL JOURNEY CONNECTION

The underlying thesis of this book is that there is a connection between the practices, methodologies, even the goals of shamanism, Santería, Wicca, charisma, and Christian mysticism. This common characteristic is the trance or altered state of consciousness as the means to encounter the supernatural realm.

In shamanism the trance state or ecstasy is the doorway opening up contact with the spirits and "souls of the dead." Without the trance state there would be no shamanism. As discussed in chapter one, Shamanism is the natural outgrowth of animism, the primitive notion that all of nature, animate and inanimate, is alive with spirit and/or soul. Because of being alive, they can be communicated with, appeased, even worshipped. Shamanism is the institutionalization of animism into a religious system.

In Santería is the celebratory bembe, the drumming party, where dancers enter into a trance state and are possessed by one or more orishas. In addition, at the heart of Santería is spiritism, introduced under the influence of the French Spiritist Allan Kardec, which relies on mediums and their séances.

In Wicca is path-working or soul journeying into the Otherworld, which also depends upon the trance state. Most books on Wicca, as well as works on shamanism, will come complete with how-to descriptions of methods to reach altered states of consciousness.[1]

Charisma, while largely sharing an orthodox Christian theology, may well have certain elements of worship and praise that transform it into something much less biblically Christian. Christians for centuries have had their "psalms, hymns, and spiritual songs" (see Ephesians 5:19 and Colossians 3:10) minus the hypnotic, mind numbing, rock oriented music and the moving to the beat while singing "seven words eleven times" in order to "feel the Spirit."

Christian mysticism, perhaps best described as contemplative prayer, with its visualizations, focusing, breath control, inner looking, concentration, and meditation, all accompanied by mellow mood music, crosses the line from biblically oriented prayer into a light, medium, or deep trance state. And in that altered state of consciousness, the practitioner often is waiting to hear voices from some exalted being or otherwise have a direct interaction with God.

These points are clear and based upon literature that comes from proponents of all of the above.

MY PERSONAL EXPERIENCE[2]

I have written a variety of essays about charisma and Christian mysticism, and that material deserves a degree of expansion here. I am an evangelical Christian, with a Reformed Theology, who accepts as legitimate the charismatic gifts as listed in Romans 12 and 1 Corinthians 12. Therefore, this topic is far more personal than are the studies of shamanism, Santería, and Wicca.

---

1   The active, aware, reality-centered mind poses a barrier to those who would enter a trance state, thus the need to bypass, suppress, or otherwise suspend the conscious or normal state of mind.

2   Kent's experiences as a pastor of a charismatic church were described in the previous chapter; however, this book is composed of a series of essays that appeared first on the website www.earthenvesseljournal.com, so there is some necessary overlap.

During the 1970s period when I was the pastor of a charismatic, non-denominational church, there were occasions when our praise band created an atmosphere where a trance-like state could have been experienced by some of the worshippers. Some people would "fall out" or be "slain in the Spirit" – phrases we had picked up from Pentecostals. What happened in a congregant's mind when such events occurred is beyond my knowing. In retrospect, I am now suspicious.

One place I am sure was spiritually unsafe was the People's Temple in San Francisco, pastored by the infamous Jim Jones, who eventually led his congregation to a mass suicide. When I visited there, I experienced a spiritual atmosphere that felt heavy, even dangerous. The result of regular participation in that venue certainly might have yielded some kind of takeover of heart and mind.

Then came the church growth movement in the 1980s, with which I became acquainted through conferences hosted by Fuller Theological Seminary in Pasadena, California. There I heard C. Peter Wagner and John Wimber talk about creating a "worshipful" time when people would be enthralled with the presence of the Spirit of God. The troubling parts of their recommendations were the techniques used in order to reach such enthrallment. Wimber carefully explained that this depended on music, lighting, and the "manipulative urgings" of the praise leader. The elements required were a crowd, hopefully young, who were used to getting into high and exciting worship; then the band, the beat, and the cheer leader (my phrase) created an atmosphere of anticipation, for perhaps forty-five minutes, then "God would show up." For other situations, such as when older folk made up most of the congregation and thus were not used to contemporary praise and worship styles, a longer period was required. And if done properly, then "God would show up."

In situations when what is described above came together, then indeed the "Spirit" would manifest and anything might happen: people screaming, falling on the floor, dancing around, and babbling in what were thought to be unknown tongues, all while the band played on ever louder.[3] The music took over, while the lyrics, as simple and vapid as could be, went on and on. As might be expected, when this sort of worship becomes the norm, the norm does not satisfy for long. Something more is always desired, and there is always something new coming along.

The scenes that I witnessed over the years reminded me of the days when I visited the Hare Krishna Temple on Fredrick Street in San Francisco during the winter of 1967. There I had to sit through the Kirtans that lasted an hour and a half and were composed of three separate chants, each lasting about thirty minutes. The experience transported one into the ozone with the chanting, drumming, and playing of other instruments, such as finger cymbals.

JUMPING TO REDDING, KANSAS CITY, AND TORONTO

Many churches have opted for the contemporary music model with loud praise music, but something more was needed for those who belonged to churches that were constantly ready for new and better revelations.

That "something more' may have started in Toronto before catching on in various other parts of North America: Brownsville (Pensacola) Florida, Lakeland, Florida, IHOP in Kansas City, Kansas, and Bethel Church in Redding, California, among other places.[4] Now there was more, meaning more miracles, such as teeth getting capped with gold, feathers floating down from the ceiling, swirling clouds with gold-like glitter

---

3   Rather than cite churches, places, and dates, this paragraph is a composite summary.

4   Rodney Howard-Browne of South Africa brought the "anointing" to the Toronto Airport Vineyard Church and the "Laughing Revival" was on. Go to www.earthenvesseljournal.com for my essay on the claimed revival, entitled "The Anointing, The Anointing, The Anointing."

mixed in, and people falling down in trance-like states lasting hours, sometimes days. Added to that was "soaking prayer" where people simply lay on the floor and "soaked" for hours and hours.[5] These people often afterward reported meeting angels, saints, or even Jesus himself, while they lay in their strange condition.

What is the nature of these phenomena? Do I imagine that Christians could be fooled into accepting as genuine that which was from the dark side? The short answer is, "Yes," but it is more complicated than that. Some of the confusion may be attributed to inaccurate understandings of how God works. Charismatics and Pentecostals (as well as others) tend to be accepting of more than they should, and everyone loves miracles. Many crave proof that God is real and involved in their lives. We are vulnerable to deception, and the most vulnerable is the one who insists he or she is not. Back in my own charismatic days, if someone said, "Thus saith the Lord," we were all ears. Our discernment often proved to be fallible or completely absent.

With over forty years of pastoral ministry behind me, experience tells me that not only are born-again Christians susceptible to deception, but not all who say they are Christians actually are. Every experienced pastor knows about false conversion. The church is a public venue, and anyone may walk through the front door. Doctrine and theology are often scoffed at by people who would rather rely on emotional and sensory experiences and what is currently in vogue, and thus a necessary element of discernment is missing. Not all that is spiritual is necessarily of God. Jesus' warning to the apostles is as valid today as it was then: "For false christs and false prophets will arise and perform great signs and wonders, so as to

---

5   Knowledge of this comes from watching online videos and speaking with acquaintances who have participated in it. Soaking is a word that does not communicate well, but it was not praying. Soaking was essentially lying on the floor, sometimes somewhat conscious but sometimes not.

lead astray, if possible, even the elect" (Matthew 24:24).

A LARGER CONNECTION – POWER AND ASSURANCE

Power has long been noted as a prime mover for those engaged in occult practices. Magic is essentially the idea that people can manipulate their environment through the control of forces and energies. Attraction to magic is prompted by the desire or need to have power over people and circumstances. Divination or fortune telling is a quest for knowledge of the future, and knowledge is power.

Séances, which are crafted and convened for contact with the dead and other spiritual entities, may bring assurance that those who have "passed over" or have "transitioned" are okay. Séances may also bring hope that the grave is not the end. It is amazing and life changing to suddenly have evidence of a spirit world where the dead are not really dead but have an existence, however shadowy, after death.

Spiritualism and Spiritism are both movements that explore the afterlife and claim that the dead can be contacted, mainly by the use of the séance and through the expertise of mediums, shamans, or channellers. It is exhilarating indeed, and once a person has such experiences, he or she will not be talked out of them easily. These "spirits of the dead," however, are not really what the participants think they are. This situation is a characteristic shared by all the religious systems studied in this book.

Clearly, the elements of power and assurance are operative in shamanism, Santería, and Wicca. It is much the same with charisma and mysticism. Experiencing God,[6] seeking after miracles, having visions of traveling to heaven, conversing with

---

6   Scripture has no commandment to experience God, but the Christian is to have faith in the saving work of Jesus Christ. Once in the presence of God in heaven, faith and hope will be subsumed into love. Paul, in 1 Cor. 13:13, speaks to this issue and concludes the discussion with, "So now faith, hope, and love abide, these three; but the greatest of these is love."

angels, being given prophecies concerning the future – could it be the quest for power and assurance? While living by faith in the God and Father of our Lord Jesus Christ has never been a simple thing for anyone, it is what we are called to do, and anything much beyond that borders on the unbiblical and dangerous.

In the garden, Satan's pitch to Eve was to experience knowledge and, by extension, power. The devil's argument was convincing, and he successfully closed the sale, overwhelming Eve and then Adam as well. Power and knowledge are potent lures to draw many away from simple trust in the Triune God.

Those who promote practices such as soaking prayer and who seek unusual manifestations such as feathers and gold dust drifting down from the rafters would say that such are evidence of the presence of the Holy Spirit and power. By implication, the average church thus appears to be devoid of the Holy Spirit, if such wonderful and strange phenomena are not evident. They might then say, "There is no power there, no Holy Spirit power." Power, used by some in regard to the exercise of certain spiritual gifts such as prophecy, healing, and miracles, may be the subject around which significant confusion arises.

JESUS AND SPIRITUAL POWER

Jesus warned about troubling times to come, especially toward the close of His ministry.

In Matthew 24, when Jesus' disciples asked Him about what was ahead, His answer began with, "See that no one leads you astray." Then in verse 11 He said, "And many false prophets will arise and lead many astray." There is more in verse 24, quoted earlier: "For false christs and false prophets will arise and perform great signs and wonders, so as to lead astray, if possible, even the elect."

The devil has power and performs miracles. This was certainly true at Jim Jones' People's Temple in San Francisco. Oil dripped from the ceiling and landed on the pages of open

Bibles; "angel's wings" brushed the shoulders and heads of worshippers; the smell of the "sweet savor" of the Lord wafted through the air; and unseen hands clasped the up-raised hands of congregants. I experienced all of this myself on two separate occasions. The devil certainly does the miraculous, but mere power displays are proof of nothing other than spiritual forces at work.

The Apostle Paul warned the Ephesian elders that "after my departure fierce wolves will come in among you, not sparing the flock; and from among your own selves will arise men speaking twisted things, to draw away the disciples after them" (Acts 20:29-30).

There is more in Scripture to support the argument that not all supernatural events are godly and holy.

CHARISMA NEED NOT BE CONNECTED TO SHAMANISM, SANTERÍA, AND WICCA

At issue here is the altered states of consciousness that can be produced in some forms of worship. If well-educated and aware people can fall into religions such as shamanism, Santería, and Wicca, certainly those in the pews are also vulnerable, so a cautionary word is of value.

After considering all the examples given throughout this book, it should be clear that it is in the trance state that people get hooked into what is fundamentally evil. Once the miraculous is encountered it is very difficult not to buy the whole package. The reason is that our natural and normal mental and emotional guards are down in the trance state, leaving us open to the possibility of being invaded or possessed by non-benign entities. And let me be abundantly clear now: there is only one Holy Spirit and He always and only glorifies, testifies, and reveals the person and work of Jesus Christ.

My concern is also for those in the broad Christian community, those who are exploring contemplative or centering prayer, on the one hand, or those who are tempted by such practices as soaking prayer and sozo ministry, because these are practices that can move one into a trance state much like what happens in shamanism, Santería, or Wicca.

Again, one approach that might be helpful to increase discernment about the biblical "safety" of a proposed practice is to ask and endeavor to answer whether a practice has clear and unquestioned precedent and/or warrant in the Christian Scripture.

Precedent: Do we see it in the Bible?[7] Did Jesus do it, teach it, or allow it? Do we see it in the experience of the early Church as recorded in the Bible? Some will say that the Bible can be used to condone almost anything, but this is not quite accurate. Scripture can, however, be bent and twisted. Precedent must be clear and unequivocal.

Warrant: If something is not specifically taught and/or practiced in Scripture, then there must be some kind of biblical warrant or a clear reason, based on doctrine, to accept whatever is in question, whether a practice or a doctrine. This is the more liberal test and one that therefore must be more carefully examined.

One of the factors that has led to so much mischief and deception is the claim that we are now living in the "last days," those days just before the second coming of Jesus.[8] The argument states that events now occurring appear to be those prophesied for the last days, including bizarre weather patterns, earthquakes, wars, etc., and that we are now "off the charts" of existing biblical revelation, meaning that God is doing and revealing things now among His people that are

---

7   Examples such as David dancing naked after a military victory, Saul's dancing with the prophets, Daniel's swoon, and Paul's being "caught up to the third heaven" are more fully presented in Section 2-4 in, "Biblical Considerations."

8   No one knows when Jesus will return, and it seems that nearly every generation in the past hundred years or so has forecasted that theirs would be the last. These prognostications are usually based on political and economic events.

not mentioned in the Bible. How convenient! Therefore, anything goes, especially if promoted by a powerful, charismatic leader with enormous resources and reputation. The claim for extra-biblical revelation is fraudulent and disingenuous, and upon hearing it, one is best served by heading for the nearest exit.

CONCLUSION AND SUMMARY

The primary connection between shamanism, Santería, Wicca, and some aspects of Christianity is the trance state, ecstasy, altered state of consciousness, or passive state of mind – these terms being synonymous. Such a state makes possible the invasion of demonic spirits into the mind and body of the person in the trance. In the first three religions just mentioned, the trance state is precisely what is sought, although it mostly goes unrecognized. However, it is not the normal goal of charisma.

The research that preceded the writing of this book indicates that few, if any, persons sought to deliberately involve themselves with evil or demonic beings. There are certainly those who do so; one only has to examine the "palo" sects of Santería to see this. Their motivation is power, and the devil is considered to be very powerful. People are regularly deceived and thus captured; however, many have later come out of such deception, as there is always hope in the grace and love of God displayed to us so clearly in Jesus Christ.

SECTION TWO

This section consists of material that relates sometimes directly and at other times tangentially to the major chapters of Section One. Again, each of these began as a stand-alone essay, and some were published in Earthen Vessel Publishing's online journal: www.earthenvesseljournal.com.

YOGA
AND ZEN

The holy people and gurus of Hinduism value and depend upon trance states. Yoga means "union," and the union desired is with deity, however they choose to define that deity. Unsurprisingly, that union takes place by means of the trance state.

Buddhism flows out of Hinduism, so there is considerable overlapping between the two. Our primary focus in this chapter will be on Buddhism, but in many ways the two may be considered as one in actual practice.

In early Buddhist Scriptures, the Buddha explained the Noble Eightfold Way.[1] These are right view, right intention, right speech, right action, right livelihood, right effort, right mindfulness, and right concentration.[2] It is this last one, right concentration, where the subject of the trance state surfaces.

In Buddhism, there are four levels of trance that help a person achieve right concentration. Starting out, when a monk is free from passions and evil thoughts, he then attains to and abides in the first trance of joy and pleasure. When a monk ceases reasoning and investigation, in a state of internal serenity, with the mind fixed on one point, he attains to and abides in the second trance of joy and pleasure arising from concentration. Abiding in and attaining the third trance means the

---

1   Mircea Eliade, *From Primitives to Zen*, Harper & Row, New York, 1967, pages 574-575.

2   Concentration is synonymous with meditation in Buddhism.

monk, with equanimity and indifference towards joy, abides mindful and self-possessed, and with his body experiences pleasure that the noble ones call "dwelling with equanimity, mindful and happy." Finally, dispelling pleasure and pain, and even before the disappearance of elation and depression, he attains and abides in the fourth trance, where the monk is without pleasure or pain and is in right concentration.

It is obvious, therefore, that Buddhist practices incorporate, indeed rely upon, the trance state. It is astonishing to note the process: free from passions – really? No evil thoughts – is this possible? No reasoning or investigation – blind and defenseless is better? Can the mind be truly fixed on one point? Can a person – and is it healthy and right – be indifferent to joy? Is the goal of existence to be without pleasure? To dismiss emotions and reasoning, both key functions of the brain, one would have to literally be outside of his or her mind, and this is, indeed, the trance state.

Few practitioners of Yoga and Zen would deny that an altered state of consciousness is what they routinely seek; only those who perceive of Yoga as no more than a form of physical exercise might miss seeing the deeper goals. Serious devotees of both Yoga and Zen are well schooled in the techniques for detaching or removing themselves from the normal or usual state of mind in order to be at a place or state of mind other than that which is normative.

DO YOGA AND ZEN PRACTITIONERS ENCOUNTER SPIRITS?

While both Yoga and Zen utilize meditation, concentration, and focusing, and while both may use mantras, koans,[3] and various forms of music, it is not common for practitioners of Yoga and Zen to encounter spiritual entities while in states of

---

3 A koan is a riddle without a solution, and, in concentrating on the koan, one's mind may be altered to the point that a passive state of mind is achieved.

trance. It would actually be more common in Yoga than Zen, but much more so in shamanism, Santería, and neo-pagan disciplines like Wicca.

Despite the fact that no mention is made by Yoga and Zen practitioners of meeting the various spirit guides, spirit animals, fairies, elves, and gods and goddesses in their trances, danger lurks nevertheless. While in trance states, Hindus and Buddhists come upon more than nothingness during deep meditation.[4] Their western counterparts have similar experiences when learning how to enter advanced states of meditation or concentration.

The "more" mentioned above refers to spiritual entities of some kind. Over the years I have talked with persons who have encountered them while deep in meditation. On occasion the person is exhilarated, other times frightened. To discover the actual existence of "otherness" can be captivating, as I have expressed a number of times, even if the spiritual encounter was thought to be taking place only in one's mind.[5] Regardless of whether a separate reality exists in these situations, when actual spiritual beings are encountered and even conversed with, then biblically speaking, such encounters fall into the demonic realm.

THE WORK OF THE HOLY SPIRIT AND THE CHRISTIAN WORLDVIEW

The Christian worldview, clearly delineated in the Chris-

---

4   Americanized forms of Yoga and Zen, while not relying upon their traditional forms, may nevertheless move toward entering or attempting to enter into trance states despite the sanitizing of the religious forms. The movement from physical exercise to efforts to achieve an ASC depends largely on the goals of the teacher.

5   There is a debate among those acquainted with trance states as to whether what is experienced is taking place within the mind or if there is "astral travel" to actual places outside the head or mind. I have no fixed opinion on the matter; both are the result of a demonic deception. I do, however, suspect it is all within the mind.

tian Scriptures, is that there is one Holy Spirit. God's Holy Spirit always points to the person and work of Jesus Christ. The Holy Spirit testifies to the fact that Jesus is the promised Messiah of Israel, is both God and man, and that as the sinless sacrificial Lamb of God, He died to make atonement for sin.[6] The Holy Spirit's testimony continues that on the third day He was raised from the dead, is now seated at the right hand of the Father, and will come again to judge the living and the dead. The Holy Spirit brings honor and glory to Jesus, who is Lord of lords and King of kings.

The gods, goddesses, guides, angels, familiars and other spirit beings encountered in the trance states are not representatives of the Triune God, but rather they are emissaries of Satan, the devil, who, in his envy of the Creator God desires to receive worship due to the Father Almighty alone and attempts to divert it to himself. Behind shamanistic religions like Santería, Wicca, and all spiritual and religious disciplines that depend on the altered state of consciousness, is a dreadful evil presence who seeks to be honored, worshipped, and adored in place of the true and living God.

---

6   Sin is a word, derived from Latin but with traces of meaning from other languages, that essentially has to do with guilt, that inner sense of having done something morally wrong.

MEDITATION

Meditation is something that is common to most, if
not all, the world's faiths. Some form of meditation
is common to Buddhism (especially Zen), Hindu-
ism (including Yoga), Sufism, Islam, Judaism (particularly Kabbalah, an occult-oriented offshoot of Judaism), and even some
forms of Christianity. The essential Christian understanding of
meditation can be broken down into three parts: a conscious
focus on who God is, what God has done, and what God has
said. The word "meditate" is found in most English New Testaments in Luke 21:14 and 1 Timothy 4:15. The Greek word in
both passages is meletao (in Luke a preposition comes before
meletao). The word means to consider or think about. In the
Luke passage Jesus is speaking: "Settle it therefore in your
minds not to meditate beforehand how to answer..." Clearly
Jesus has thinking in mind. In the 1 Timothy 4:15 passage, Paul
is giving instruction to his young disciple Timothy: "Practice
these things, devote yourself to them, so that all may see your
progress." Paul urges Timothy to "practice," with meletao being
the word translated as practice. This gives us an idea about the
ancient meaning of meditation, which is mindful, conscious,
and reality-oriented thinking.

In the Old Testament, meditate or meditation is found in
nineteen places, mostly in the Book of Psalms. For example,
in Joshua 1:8, God says to Joshua, who is Moses' second in
command, "This Book of the Law shall not depart from your

mouth, but you shall meditate on it day and night." Here Joshua is instructed to focus on or think about the Word of God. In Psalm 119:15 we find, "I will meditate on your precepts and fix my eyes on your ways;" and verse 23 of that Psalm reads, "your servant will meditate on your statutes."

In Scripture there is nothing about an emptying or clearing of the mind. The mind, the thoughts, or the reasoning process are a far cry from the kind of meditation found in all other religious practices.

Christianity does not view the mind as an enemy or thinking as an obstacle. Scripture says nothing about putting the mind into neutral so that the divine can therefore communicate with a person.

It is true that Teresa of Avila and John of the Cross, among others, including contemporary people in the Christian fraternity, speak of a mystical form of meditation that encourages the blank state of mind, but this is neither biblical nor mainstream Christian practice.

Meditation or its popular designation, contemplative prayer, may seem good and may bring a measure of peacefulness, but it is still not the same as biblical meditation.

Why my concern with this subject? My answer is that in the passive, altered, or trance state of conscious there is a very great danger.

MY OWN FINDINGS

In the Haight-Ashbury district of San Francisco, during the days when, due to the Beatles' influence, Transcendental Meditation was all the rage, I met many people who became adept at this meditation form. When their normal boundaries and critical defenses of mind and spirit cracked under deep meditation, however, demonic spirits invaded them. Yes, these people opened themselves up to demonic possession. This was often confirmed to me years afterward when people thus affected would arrive at the church I pastored and request deliverance from such unclean spirits.

Two illustrative instances come to mind.

On one occasion, a young hippie I met on the street in the Haight stopped me and asked if I could help get voices out of his head that continually yelled at him. We retreated to a little park on Haight Street just east of the main section, and I asked him when the voices started. Having been trained in psychology, I wanted to know if the voices had been around a long time or was it something new – chronic or acute. He told me the voices started, little by little, at his initiation into TM. He said the spirit of the founder of the movement came to him and began advising him on various things, and as time went on, the advise turned into demands and threats. He would try to meditate to block out the voices, but this only served to make matters worse. At that point, sadly, I did not know enough about casting out of demons then to help him. I did pray for him, gave him a New Testament, and urged him to trust in Jesus.

Years later, in the normal course of doing deliverance ministry, which is the casting out of demons, I encountered something similar. A man who had been initiated into TM described the same experience as the young hippie: the voices, the demands, and the confusion. To the best of my understanding the person was in his right mind. This time we were able to cast demons out of him, and one had the name of the founder of TM. When I later contacted this man, he reported that he no longer felt compelled to meditate and that the voices had ceased entirely.

That this occurs may come as a surprise to many; it certainly did to me. Were it not for the possibility of attracting demonic spirits while in a trance state, even if it is thought to be a form of contemplative prayer, I would never have challenged the idea that meditation can lead to an altered state of consciousness. But the fact is, when the walls come down in a deep meditative state, an unwelcome and unwanted invasion is possible, even probable.

SOUL ?

I n 2002, Evangelical Press in the UK published Kent's book entitled, *Why I am a Christian*. Chapter 11 is "Soul Confusion." The concept of the soul is one of the chief philosophical underpinnings of religions discussed in this present book. Indeed, shamanism, Santería, Wicca, charisma, and Christian mysticism are deeply indebted to the Greek dualistic concept of the soul.[1] Despite that, it produces considerable theological and spiritual confusion among all who discuss it, and few know the origins of their own closely held ideas.

The following is the entire chapter, "Soul Confusion," from *Why I am a Christian*, followed by some further comments, all with the hope of clarifying this crucial and confusing concept.

SOUL CONFUSION

The March 16, 1999 *Larry King Live*, an American television chat show, featured five panelists: Robert Thurman, professor of Buddhism studies at Columbia University; Marianne

---

1   Greek dualism posited a battle between good and evil, a war of equals, in which all that is matter or material is evil, and all that is immaterial, i.e., the mind, spirit, and soul, is good. Thus Greek dualism did not hold to an integrated view of the human being. The Greek version of "person" became incorporated into what is sometimes called the Western mindset as opposed to the Eastern mindset that viewed a person as an integrated whole. The latter view is reflected in the Bible, in both Old and New Testaments. See more on this in footnote #3.

Williamson, New Age author and spokesperson for the spir-
itistically channeled Course in Miracles; Rabbi David Aaron,
expert on and proponent of Kabbalah, an occult/mystical/
gnostic interpretation of Judaism; Deepak Chopra, charismatic spokesperson for a popular version of Hindu monistic
thought; and Franklin Graham, head of Samaritans Purse, a
Christian humanitarian organization, and son of Billy Graham,
the renowned American evangelist.

WHAT IS THE SOUL?

Though these five differed on many points, they seemed
to reach a consensus in understanding "soul." In fact, Deepak
Chopra voiced agreement with Graham's understanding of the
soul. We have long heard Billy Graham say words like: "You
have a soul and it will go to heaven or hell when you die."

According to this idea, the soul is a mysterious, spiritual
and immortal part of the human being that leaves the cold,
dead body at death. Those on Larry King's programme who
believed in some form of reincarnation were able to agree
together about the soul though, from their own traditions,
they might have used other symbols to express the same thing.

Due to a revival of Geek philosophy in the fourth and fifth
centuries A.D., Greek dualism infiltrated the Christian Church
mainly through the work of Thomas Aquinas and his Summa
Theologica, which became the fountainhead of Catholic theology throughout the Dark Ages. Greek dualistic thought posits
the theory that the mind, spirit and soul are good, even divine,
while on the other hand, the body, flesh and matter are bad,
the repository of evil. So it was the soul that mattered, the soul
that needed saving; the body was simply a temporary prison
for the soul.

SOUL AND SELF

Confusion concerning the nature of the soul has a powerful influence among the people of Mill Valley where I minis-

ter. Though the doctrine is not biblical, and is absent from the teaching of the early church, the idea that the soul is the focus of evangelistic efforts persists in many Christian traditions. Franklin Graham was concerned about the soul. He should have been concerned about the whole person; body, mind, soul, and spirit.

So many in my community believe in reincarnation that Graham's doctrine on the soul would not be troublesome for them. The soul? Well, they say, it needs purifying and experiences endless lifetimes anyway. These people do not like to think that they will be resurrected to stand before the judgment of God. "My soul" is one thing; "myself" is another.

TOTAL RESURRECTION

The biblical doctrine is one of bodily resurrection, not the floating away of an immortal soul. We are whole, integrated beings, though the Bible writers spoke variously of mind, heart, body, flesh, spirit and soul for the sake of emphasis. A person is all of these and more, a whole being responsible to God in the totality and indivisibility of his nature. What we are in total will be raised from the dead, either to eternal life or eternal death. We do not have immortality in and of ourselves. This truth is found in 1 Corinthians 15:53: "For this corruptible must put on incorruption, and this mortal must put on immortality" (NKJV).

Soul confusion must be countered by the truth of the resurrection, even if it means parting from long-established ways of thinking and preaching. Let us not give the unconverted comfort by implying that they have only some ethereal soul to be concerned about.

ADDITIONAL COMMENTARY

Probably more Christians than not hold to the idea of a soul that is somehow inside the body and survives biological death. This is understandable, because the Church in the fourth century incorporated the idea into its theology, and it has remained ever since.

Flourishing in the fourth century was a revival of Greek philosophy, mainly dualism of the Neo-Platonic or Neo-Aristotelian varieties.[2] Over a millennium later the reformers such as Martin Luther and John Calvin, both ministers (priests) in the Roman Catholic Church, retained their Church's doctrine of the soul, despite expounding salvation by grace through faith alone. Only the more radical reformers, the Anabaptists, looked for their theological foundations further back in history before Augustine of Hippo (A.D. 354-430), the great Pauline theologian, who incorporated the construct of the separate existence of the soul in the human being. The famous Augustine, one of my heroes of the Church, nevertheless was steeped in Greek philosophy and blended the dualistic concept of the soul into his Christian views. Thomas Aquinas (A.D. 1225-1274), another great theologian, then included the Greek influenced doctrine of the soul in his Summa Theologica, minus the portion about the transmigration and pre-existence of the soul that was common to Greek philosophy.

The Christian Protestant denominations originating out of the Reformation inherited the concept of the soul. From Luther comes the Lutheran denominations; from John Calvin and John Knox come the Reformed and Presbyterian churches, followed by the Congregational churches, the Anglican Church, and by extension both American Episcopal and Methodist churches, plus all the offshoots from these denominations. Not all the Baptists, who followed the Anabaptists, rejected the Greek

---

2   Dualism, among other things, viewed the body as bad, even evil, while the mind, spirit, soul, were good and connected to the divine. The body then became the prison house of the soul, which supposedly pre-existed and entered human bodies, transmigrated or left them upon death. The Eastern concepts of karma and reincarnation are dependent upon this understanding of soul.

influenced soul view, but many did. Pentecostals and charismatics hold a variety of concepts about the soul.

A BRIEF LOOK AT BIBLICAL PASSAGES HAVING TO DO WITH THE SOUL

We first encounter the word "soul" in Genesis 2:7: "Then
he LORD God formed the man of dust from the ground and
breathed into his nostrils the breath of life, and the man
became a living creature." And the reader would be correct in
protesting, where is the word "soul?" The version quoted is
the English Standard Version (hereafter ESV) and has replaced
"soul" with "creature." And why? Because "creature" is a better
rendering of the Hebrew *nephesh* than soul. The point is that
God created a human being.

The King James Version (hereafter KJV) and older English
versions of the Bible translate nephesh as "soul," and so the
term has stuck. Furthermore, soul has come to acquire something close to the idea of "ghost," and not because of anything
biblical. And in fact, in Job 11:20 and Jeremiah 15:9, the KJV
translates the Hebrew nephesh with ghost.

In Deuteronomy 6:5 we find the greatest of the commandments: "You shall love the LORD your God with all your heart
and with all your soul and with all your might." The Hebrew
word for soul here is from nephesh. The point of the commandment, however, means that we are to love God with all
of us, and thus the bringing together of three words that were
commonly used to describe different aspects or characteristics of all that is human – heart, soul, might.[3]

Many Christians, including editors of biblical texts, unrea-
sonably retain how the KJV translated many words, due to
the extreme, yet appropriate popularity of that version of the

---

3   Jesus quotes Deuteronomy 6:5 and inserts the word "mind" along
with heart, soul, and strength. See Mark 12:30 and Luke 10:27. Thus Jesus
interprets the fulfilling of the greatest commandment to include the mind;
thus love of God is conscious and thoughtful.

Bible; therefore, the word "soul" pops up frequently in the Old Testament. But it means creature, person, or living being, and it does not refer to something ethereal and separate from a body. It is better said that a human being *is* a soul. To say a human being *has* a soul is not a biblical construct. And those who disagree I advise to investigate the issue and not to simply rely on tradition.

There are literally dozens of passages in the Old Testament where it is clear that the English word soul really means person. For the purposes of this book, two examples will be given that are characteristic of the lot. The first is from Exodus 1:5, and the KJV is, "And all the souls that came out of the loins of Jacob were seventy souls: for Joseph was in Egypt already." Two times the word "souls" appears, and in both cases the Hebrew word is nephesh. Now the same verse in the ESV: "All the descendants of Jacob were seventy persons; Joseph was already in Egypt" (Exodus 1:5). In one instance, nephesh is translated "descendants" and in the second "persons." The ESV gives the most natural of the translations and is more accurately reflective of the Hebrew writer's mindset.

The second example is from Psalm 6:3-4, and the KJV is, "My soul is also sore vexed: but thou, O LORD, how long? Return, O LORD, deliver my soul: oh save me for thy mercies' sake." In both cases soul is nephesh. The same verse in the ESV reads, "My soul also is greatly troubled. But you, O LORD--how long? Turn, O LORD, deliver me for the sake of your steadfast love." Nephesh is the Hebrew word translated "soul" in "my soul" and "me" in "deliver me." In the first instance the ESV translators have the emotional experience of the writer in mind – King David's emotional state of mind to be exact – and so the term "soul" meets the literary requirement to better convey emotion. In the second instance "me" is more appropriate, as David is directly referring to his person. This second instance from the Psalms illustrates a wide range of translation possibilities, but "soul" speaks to us in a poetic manner.

The Greek translation of the Hebrew Scripture known as the Septuagint or LXX is a translation made by Jewish scholars in Alexandria Egypt in the early part of the second century before Christ. In it, psyche is used in place of nephesh in both passages, Exodus 1:5 and Psalm 6:3-4, and is consistently the case throughout the translation.

Turning our attention now to the English versions of the New Testament, we see that psyche is sometimes translated "soul." With the exception of the Gospel of Luke and the Book of Acts, the New Testament was written by Jews who inherited the Jewish understanding of the soul. Jews did not believe, in complete distinction from the Greeks, that the soul was anything other than the whole person. Old and even new translations of the New Testament tend to pull toward the KJV and translate psyche as soul. Again, we are looking at tradition.

Let us consider a couple of examples. One is Matthew 2:20: "Saying, Arise, and take the young child and his mother, and go into the land of Israel: for they are dead which sought the young child's life" (KJV). "Life" is psyche, so the KJV used the proper word, thus revealing that the KJV translators knew the correct translation. The ESV also has "life" here. We will remember that psyche is the Greek equivalent for the Hebrew nephesh.

A second example is Matthew 10:39: "He that findeth his life shall lose it; and he that loseth his life for my sake shall find it" (KJV). "Life" in both places is psyche.

Mark 3:4 is helpful: "And he saith unto them, Is it lawful to do good on the sabbath days, or to do evil? to save life, or to kill?" Here "save life" uses psyche for life and is the antonym for "kill." Obviously, Jesus has in mind a person and not a ghost, soul, or something else of an ethereal nature, which, according to some, could not be killed anyway.

And this is the problem with importing into the Judaeo/Christian Scripture the concept of a soul that does not die or cannot be extinguished. The biblical worldview is resurrection. Jesus was resurrected; even He had no soul that survived the crucifixion. Furthermore, when Jesus cried out, "Father, into your hands I commit my spirit!" (Luke 23:46), "spirit" in the sentence is from the Greek pneuma and can be translated spirit, breath, or wind. It was essentially an idiom, a statement that would have been well understood by those who heard Him and that meant simply, "Father, as I am now dying I trust in You" – a final confession of faith.

Let us close with 1 Corinthians 15:45. First the KJV: "The first man Adam was made a living soul; the last Adam was made a quickening spirit." Soul is psyche and spirit pneuma. The ESV translates it, "The first man Adam became a living being; the last Adam became a life-giving spirit." Adam was a person, not something without a body. Jesus is the last Adam, the one who brought life and not death.

The evidence is plentiful: the Scripture knows nothing of a separate and immortal soul that alone needs saving. In Santería, Wicca, and other religions indebted to shamanistic/animistic ideas, the souls of the dead supposedly contact the living, or so it is mistakenly understood. Those who hold to such ideas are indeed contacting real entities, but instead of these being the souls of former living persons, they are demonic, evil spirits. We see how this grave error is at least partially founded on a faulty concept of soul.

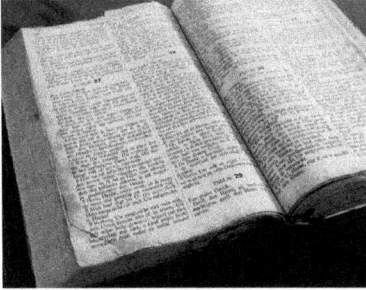

BIBLICAL MATTERS

J acob, Saul, David, Isaiah, Daniel, Jesus, Peter, Paul, and John: didn't these kings, prophets, and apostles experience trance states? Or, did they not at least engage in forms of worship similar to what is seen in charismatic and Pentecostal churches? Some advocates of such forms will make these appeals. Therefore, it will be instructive to look at each biblical personage named above to see whether their experiences fall into the category of a trance state or state of ecstasy as observed in shamanic, Santerían, Wiccan, mystical, or charismatic/Pentecostal worship.

JACOB

Jacob had a dream while camped out in the desert in a region known as the Negeb, west of the Dead Sea (Genesis 28:10-22). In the dream Jacob saw a flight of stairs that stretched from the earth to heaven. Angels were ascending and descending on it, and above the ladder Jacob saw the LORD, who identified himself as "the God of Abraham your father and the God of Isaac" (v. 13). God confirmed to Jacob the promise that He had made to Abraham and Isaac: the land Jacob was lying on would belong to him and his offspring. That is the story; now we consider the issue, was Jacob in a trance state at the time? And, was the stairway, sometimes translated "ladder," connected with shamanistic motifs?

Consider the dreaming and sleeping; they are just that and

no more. Neither involved a trance, not even a light trance state. Dreaming and sleeping are natural and require only the ordinary physiological processes of the body to occur. In other words, no special ceremonies, rituals, or other mechanisms are employed. There is nothing unusual about Jacob's sleeping; however, while everyone dreams, Jacob's was obviously more than a dream. God directly intervened and revealed Himself to Jacob, and this is not ordinary.

Since the dreaming occurred while sleeping, there was nothing in the way of the ecstatic that might have prompted the dreaming. There was no meditating, concentrating, centering, balancing, chanting, deep breathing, and so on – only dreaming while asleep.

Missionaries tell stories about God appearing to people in dreams, and the content of the communication was the truth that Jesus is Messiah and Savior. It is common now to read that Muslims, in particular, have become Christians via a dream. I have talked with people who have experienced that, both during my days of ministry in the Haight-Ashbury District of San Francisco in the 1960s and more recently. In no circumstance was there anything approaching an attempt to enter an altered state of consciousness.

SAUL

Saul was the first person to be anointed king over Israel (the story is in 1 Samuel 10 and following.) He was not chosen to be king because of his godliness, nor did he carefully follow the Law of God. His behavior resulted in God chastising him on several occasions (see 1 Samuel 13:12-13, 15:11-23).

Saul became murderously jealous of David who had served him faithfully. Saul's behavior was so despicable that God rejected him (see 1 Samuel 15:10-11), and David was anointed king instead, thus bringing about a power struggle between the two.

Immediately after Samuel anointed Saul as king, Saul

encountered a group of prophets and began to prophesy with them. This was quite unusual, so much so that the saying, "Is Saul also among the prophets?" was coined (1 Samuel 10:12). It is not clear what Saul actually did to temporarily earn the status of a prophet. It is also not clear who the prophets in the account were or what their prophesying looked like or what the content was. One thing is certain; there is no mention of Saul or any of the prophets entering into a trance state.

There is also Saul's visit to the medium at Endor (see 1 Samuel 28). The background to the story involves the dreaded Philistine nation declaring war on Israel. The Philistines bordered Israel and were a constant thorn in their side. It was a difficult time, because Israel's spiritual and moral leader, Samuel, had just died. Coinciding with that death, it is recorded that "Saul had put the mediums and the necromancers out of the land" (1 Samuel 28:3).

The armies of Israel and the Philistines faced each other at a place called Gilboa, and "when Saul saw the army of the Philistines, he was afraid, and his heart trembled greatly" (1 Samuel 28:5). Saul, out of fear, "inquired" of the Lord, but there was no answer. Saul then negated the stand he had previously taken against the occult fortune tellers and commanded someone under his authority to find a medium he could consult. Saul was told, "Behold, there is a medium at En-dor" (1 Samuel 28:7).

Saul disguised himself and arrived after sunset at Endor. He asked, "Divine for me by a spirit and bring up for me whomever I shall name to you" (1 Samuel 28:8). The medium, however, recognized Saul and balked, so he had to assure the medium that no harm would come to her in disobeying his own the royal decree banishing the mediums from Israel.

Saul wanted the medium to bring up Samuel. During that period of history, long before, and long afterward, it was commonly held by tribes and small nation-states that the dead could communicate with the living. Saul shared that belief.

The medium did bring someone up who said he was Samuel and who proceeded to accuse Saul of unfaithfulness and disobedience toward God. At one point, Saul fell to the ground in fear.

Again, there is nothing in the account of Saul's experience to suggest he entered into anything approaching a trance state. Those Saul encountered at Endor might have been shamanistic in orientation and practice, but this does not mean such behavior is sanctioned in the Bible and therefore acceptable for future generations. Nowhere in Scripture is Saul's experience accepted as proper and to be emulated.

DAVID

There is only one instance in the life of David that has been used to justify euphoric states, and that is when he danced, apparently naked, in Jerusalem.

David had rescued the box containing the Ten Commandments, the Ark of the Covenant, from the Philistines and was escorting it back to the nation of Israel, to its new home in Jerusalem. The occasion was one of great rejoicing, because it signified that God's presence was once more with His people. The key verse is, "As the ark of the LORD came into the city of David, Michal the daughter of Saul looked out of the window and saw King David leaping and dancing before the LORD, and she despised him in her heart" (2 Samuel 6:16). Michal mocked David saying, "How the king of Israel honored himself today, uncovering himself today before the eyes of his servants' female servants, as one of the vulgar fellows shamelessly uncovers himself!" (2 Samuel 6:20). David defended himself by saying, "It was before the Lord, who chose me above your father and above all his house, to appoint me as prince over Israel, the people of the LORD – and I will make merry before the LORD" (2 Samuel 6:21).

The nature of the uncovering is not certain, and there are questions about it that scholars raise, but David's extent of nakedness is largely irrelevant to the present issue. David made "merry" as he danced and leapt around. Yes, those in trance states may dance once they are in that state or dance in order to get into that state, but that does not warrant guilt by association in this case. The text does not indicate anything other than that David was happy and celebrating, and it was a onetime event.

As to the state of dress, even if David were naked, it would not mean he was "out of his mind" but that he was careless in his exuberance. And, charismatics and Pentecostals may dance, as do many others, but not naked or in anything approaching a questionable state of undress.

What if David had been in a light trance? The day of victory over the Philistines may have been a very long, hot, and strenuous event. David may not have been fully himself. We do not know anything beyond what the text states, but we can imagine what the conditions might have been like. Then, if David had been in a bit of a fog, even delirious with joy, it would not mean that trance states are normative behavior for God's people.

DANIEL

Daniel presents a more difficult circumstance.

Daniel was taken as a young Jewish boy to Babylon to King Nebuchadnezzar's court to be a servant, about 605 B.C. After the Medo-Persian overthrow of the Babylonians, he served the Persian kings Cyrus and Darius. In the Book of Daniel in the Old Testament, chapter 10, verse 1, we find this: "In the third year of Cyrus king of Persia a word was revealed to Daniel, who was named Belteshazzar. And the word was true, and it was a great conflict. And he understood the word and had understanding of the vision." This vision probably can be dated close to 536 B.C.

Verse two of chapter 10 records that Daniel mourned for three weeks, probably because the Jews who were allowed by the Persians to return to Jerusalem were meeting considerable resistance in their attempts to rebuild their capital city. Sensitive to what was occurring there, Daniel refused to eat the special foods popular with the Persians, especially meats and wine. In addition, he would not apply lotions used to combat the dry conditions of the climate.

The vision came to him while he was standing on a bank alongside the Tigris River. Daniel does not say whether this was during the day or night, but he reported, "I lifted up my eyes and looked," and he saw what has been called the Vision of the Final Conflict, recounted in chapters 10, 11, and 12 of Daniel's prophecy.

Was Daniel's vision at all comparable to the ecstatic experiences of Santeríans, Wiccans, or of those in Christian communities involved in soaking prayer, sozo ministry, or while moving and grooving to the beat in charismatic/Pentecostal worship?

Daniel was awake and not sleeping, so there is no dream involved. He was standing, he knew where he was, and he deliberately looked up and saw a vision. There is no language to indicate that he was in a trance state. He was alone; there was no music, no chanting, nothing.

Daniel 10:16 also records that Daniel spoke to the one who was revealing the future to him. Though a full analysis of all that has been written about this event is far beyond the scope of this book, a short summary is that God revealed to Daniel what would unfold over the course of several hundred years, especially the rise of a Greek military emperor, no doubt Alexander the Great and the generals who would succeed him. Daniel is even told of the time period, some say the year, when the Messiah would be born.

The vision was outward not inward. Daniel "lifted up his eyes and looked," with no indication that he was in prayer or meditation; while he was standing on the bank of the Tigris River, the vision came to him.

Daniel was a proven prophet, and there is nothing to indicate that he was in an altered state of consciousness. Although his vision is extraordinary, it is not beyond the bounds of biblical prophecy; it is consistent with it.

One more prophet is yet to be considered before we get to Jesus and the New Testament.

ISAIAH

In the year that King Uzziah died I saw the Lord sitting upon a throne, high and lifted up, and the train of his robe filled the temple. Above him stood the seraphim. Each had six wings: with two he covered his face, and with two he covered his feet, and with two he flew. And one called to another and said: "Holy, holy, holy is the LORD of hosts; the whole earth is full of his glory!" And the foundations of the thresholds shook at the voice of him who called, and the house was filled with smoke. And I said: "Woe is me! For I am lost; for I am a man of unclean lips, and I dwell in the midst of a people of unclean lips, for my eyes have seen the King, the LORD of hosts. Isaiah 6:1-5

What a dramatic vision! In the light of the holiness of God, Isaiah saw himself for who he was, a "man of unclean lips." Isaiah understood at once the extreme qualitative distinction between himself and the God of Israel.

Was Isaiah in a trance? From the text itself the question cannot be answered, although nothing presented suggests he was in anything other than a normal state of consciousness. There is no indication he was in prayer, worship, meditation, or contemplation, and nothing implies he was even focusing on God when the vision occurred.

Throughout the Book of Isaiah, the prophet receives many messages from God. During none of these receptions is there an indication he was in an altered state of consciousness.

In the prophetic literature of the Tanakh, the Old Testament, there is nothing suggesting a prophet required a trance state to receive communication from God. Isaiah's experience was certainly extraordinary, but it was one that came to him while he was perfectly alert, conscious, and mindful.

JESUS

Immediately after His baptism, Jesus fasted forty days in the wilderness, which was followed by a series of temptations by Satan to get Him to compromise His mission. Some have insisted the fasting and temptation would have been impossible without entering into a trance state. More than that, proponents of Wicca claim that the interaction between Jesus and Satan is an example of what happens on their own journeys. Some Christians on the charisma side of the Christian family cite the conversations between Jesus and the Devil as something they also experience in times of ecstasy or soaking prayer. Considering this is now Jesus we are talking about, not a prophet or king from the Hebrew Bible, the issue becomes acute.

The account of the temptation is found in Matthew, Mark, and Luke; I will focus on Matthew's account, chapter 4, verses 1 to 11.

"Forty days" can either be taken literally as forty calendar days or more generally as a time of great trouble, as in Israel's forty years of wandering in the wilderness. However it is viewed, the time Jesus spent being tempted was not something easily endured.

Fasting might be complete or not; fasting practices varied greatly; some lasted during the day light hours only, and some did not involve a lack of water. The Gospel accounts say only that Jesus was hungry at the end of the fast.

Satan and Jesus conversed directly, as though face-to-face. Nothing is said of a vision or a trance, and this is worth noting; there is no indication that what was taking place was in or resulted from a trance-like state. On the basis of what is in the text, the temptation was real and the conversations were outward and actual, not merely inward and mental.

Twice Satan took Jesus away to another location. One was to Jerusalem, to "the pinnacle of the temple," and the other was to a "very high mountain" where Satan "showed him all the kingdoms of the world and their glory." Two possibilities may account for Satan's taking Jesus to the temple and the mountain. One, it was actual. Two, it happened only inside the mind of Jesus. My present view is that the visit to the temple and the mountain occurred in real time, that is, they were actually at the locations.

What took place in the wilderness temptation, especially in the interaction between Jesus and Satan, remains mysterious to us. The Gospel writers and the early church after them had no particular difficulty with the account, and it passed into the life of the Church with little comment. Although there have been mystics within the broad framework of the Church throughout its history, any seeking for similar experiences take place on the margins only and are most often rejected as non-normative.

It must be noted that this is the only time in Jesus' earthly incarnation when there is such an occurrence. Although the voice of the Father was audible at both the baptism by John in the Jordan River and the Mount of Transfiguration, these two events are not similar to what happened at the temptation in the wilderness and would not be remotely connected to a trance state. No, the fasting and conversation with Satan is a singular event.

Also note that Jesus never taught His disciples to desire or seek anything resembling a trance or passive state of mind. Jesus taught His disciples to pray, and He gave them a model prayer, which we call The Lord's Prayer (see Matthew 6:9-13), which is spiritual in its focus on God and grounded in everyday life.

Both within the charismatic/Pentecostal realm and for Wiccans and Santerians, disagreement exists on whether the journeys they experience occur only in the mind, or whether they occur outside the body.

THE TRANSFIGURATION

The transfiguration, recorded in Matthew 17:1-8, Mark 9:2-8, and Luke 9:28-36, occurred on a mountain in northern Galilee, probably Mt. Herman. Jesus invited Peter, James, and John to ascend the mountain with Him and at a certain place Moses and Elijah, long dead personages from the history of Israel, suddenly appeared and spoke with Jesus. During this event, Jesus' appearance changed, such that His "face shone like the sun, and his clothes became white as light" (verse 2 of Matthew 17). The word "transfigured" is a translation of the Greek word from which we get our term metamorphosis, and it essentially means to change form.

Nowhere in the telling of this event is an indication that a trance state was involved for any of the participants. Jesus engaged in conversation with three of His disciples, Peter, James, and John. Moses and Elijah, thought to represent the Law and the Prophets, also appeared and conversed with Jesus, although the content of their conversation is not recorded. Their presence was so real and tangible, Peter asked to build shelters for Jesus and the visitors. The experience troubled the disciples, and Jesus "came and touched them," apparently to comfort them.

In verse 9, Jesus told the three disciples, "Tell no one the vision, until the Son of Man is raised from the dead." The word "vision" is orama – a transliteration from Greek to English. It is found often in the Book of Acts, for instance in 9:10, 10:3, 11:5, and 16:9. It has to do with divine revelation, perhaps in a dream or day dream. There is nothing suggesting the receptor of the orama is in an ecstasy or altered state. It is a direct intervention by God. To put it another way, there is nothing "shamanistic" about biblical visions.

PETER

In the Roman city of Caesarea, situated in the northwestern part of Israel on the eastern coast of the Mediterranean Sea, lived a Roman centurion named Cornelius. He was "a devout man who feared God with all his household, gave alms generously to the people, and prayed continually to God" (Acts 10:2). He had a vision that told him his prayers had been answered and to send for a man named "Simon, who is called Peter. He is lodging with one Simon, a tanner, whose house is by the sea" (Acts 10:5-6).

Peter was visiting the home of Simon the tanner in Joppa, forty miles south of Caesarea, a city also on the Mediterranean. At noon Peter was praying on the roof of Simon's house. (It was typical of houses in that clime to use roofs as an additional room.) "And he became hungry and wanted something to eat, but while they were preparing it, he fell into a trance and saw the heavens opened and something like a great sheet descending, being let down by its four corners upon the earth" (Acts 10:10-11). In the sheet were many kinds of animals, some deemed clean by the Jews but others rejected as unclean. The experience made clear to Peter that Gentiles would be included in the "household" of God, an idea abhorrent for most Jews of that day to accept.

Peter, while praying with conscious expressions directed to God, received a message from God. To emphasize that the message was from God we find the word "trance" translated from the Greek ekstasis, which means "outside of oneself." The point of the term meant that there was a message or vision that did not arise in the mind or imagination of the receptor – in this case, Peter. In other words, what Peter saw and heard came from outside of him.

In Acts 11:5, Peter recounted what happened with Cornelius in Caesarea and used the word ekstasis in order to make it clear that God, and not he himself, had orchestrated the whole event.

There is one other place in the New Testament where ekstasis is found, in Acts 22:17, which we will examine when considering Paul. So, there are three places in the New Testament where a Greek word is translated as "trance," although in no place is such a state sought or considered necessary or exalted. Neither is the denotation nor the connotation of the English word "trance" the same as when it is used, for example, by Wiccans. The point is that, in describing their received vision or message from God, neither Peter nor Paul questioned or even described their mental or spiritual state of mind. While each was in a right and conscious mind, God chose to reveal something they could not have known otherwise.

PAUL

Paul was no mystic, but he had unusual, non-deliberate mystical experiences, and he spoke of them in Acts 22:17 and 2 Corinthians 12:1-10. First let us consider Acts 22:17-21:

> When I had returned to Jerusalem and was praying in the temple, I fell into a trance and saw him saying to me, "Make haste and get out of Jerusalem quickly, because they will not accept your testimony about me." And I said, "Lord, they themselves know that in one synagogue after another I imprisoned and beat those who believed in you. And when the blood of Stephen your witness was being shed, I myself was standing by and approving and watching over the garments of those who killed him." And he said to me, "Go, for I will send you far away to the Gentiles."

The word is again ekstasis – "trance." While Paul was in the temple praying, he received a message from God, and in his recounting of it he characterized it as a conversation. There is no question that this was a very unique and utterly spiritual communication. At the same time, apart from the word, Paul's experience bears no resemblance to the trance states found in Santería, Wicca, and many of the states associated with soaking prayer, sozo, and the swaying to drum rhythms. More important than the use of a word is Paul's, and Peter's before him, actual state of mind.

Luke would not likely have translated his word ekstasis into the modern English understanding of the word "trance," and he, a Greek and not a Jew, is the only one who uses the word ekstasis in the New Testament. This is another clue that first century Jews did not associate their praying with altered states of consciousness.

Next consider verses 2 Corinthians 12:1-4:

> I must go on boasting. Though there is nothing to be gained by it. I will go on to visions and revelations of the Lord. I know a man in Christ who fourteen years ago was caught up to the third heaven – whether in the body or out of the body I do not know, God knows. And I know that this man was caught up into paradise – whether in the body or out of the body I do not know – and he heard things that cannot be told, which man may not utter.

The apostle Paul had other visions and revelations from God, although the one spoken of above was foremost. Just after the Damascus Road experience, Paul was escorted to that city and there saw a vision of a man named Ananias coming to visit him (Acts 9:12). He also had a vision wherein God directed him to begin presenting the message of the Jewish messiah to Gentiles (Acts 22:17). While pursuing his missionary work, Paul had a vision that led him to Macedonia (Acts 16:9). When the work was particularly difficult, God gave Paul a vision that encouraged him (Acts 18:9-10). Then, while on his way to

Rome as a prisoner, his ship was caught in a severe storm, but God told Paul in a vision that no one aboard the vessel would be lost (Acts 27:23).

Paul alludes to a revelation from God about the great mystery, a mystery now revealed, which was that Gentiles would be included into the Family of God (Ephesians 3:1-6).

Paul's authority as an apostle was challenged from time to time. Paul no sooner left a city in which he had testified of salvation in Jesus Christ, than his detractors would arrive on the scene and attempt to undo all Paul's ministry had accomplished. Paul's opponents attacked him by boasting of their own supposedly superior spiritual experiences, which served as a form of credentialing. The Book of Acts describes this, and Paul wrote about it in letters such as 2 Corinthians.

To defend his ministry Paul "boasts" but only briefly. In chapter 12, verses 7 to 10, he boasts not in revelations he had received but in his weaknesses. This is where his "thorn in the flesh" comes in. Something troubled Paul, apparently a physical malady, and some think it might have been poor eyesight approaching blindness, or maybe malaria; but in any case, rather than boast of spiritual experiences, he found that God made him strong despite his physical disability.

Paul did not know Jesus in the days of His flesh and thus was not among the original Twelve that Jesus called to be His disciples. Paul was initially a serious opponent of the early Christian Church, likely because he knew that if the story the apostles were telling was true, he and the rest of the Jewish religious community were out of business. Thus it was in the midst of Paul's persecution of the Church that Jesus appeared to him while he traveled to Damascus of Syria, whereupon Paul had a profound conversion experience (see Acts chapter 9).

It was precisely because Jesus appeared to Paul, or at least spoke to him, that Paul was considered among the apostles specially and directly appointed by Jesus.

Regarding Paul's story told to the Corinthians, he said he was caught up to the "third heaven,"[1] which means the highest heaven in typical Jewish cosmology, thus Paul meant he was in the presence of or dwelling place of God. This had occurred fourteen years previously, around A.D. 42-44, likely in Tarsus of Antioch, and prior to Paul's first missionary journey. The question is, was Paul in an altered state of consciousness when he was caught up?

There is nothing in the text to clearly answer the question. Such language or phraseology was not common to the sect of the Pharisees, of which Paul was a member, and was not used in Judaism in general. The early Church knew nothing of entering into trance states, and the practice did not appear until the advent of the desert monastics in the third and fourth centuries.

Paul did not teach that Christians should do meditation, chanting, prayer mantras, or anything normally associated with altered states of consciousness, yet he made it a point to teach everything that he had learned of the life and teachings of Jesus.

For Paul and all Jews who were conversant with the Tanakh, meditation meant a conscious, alert, and thoughtful consideration of God and what God had done – a far cry from the forms of meditation, concentration, visualization, centering, and focusing that are undertaken with the intent to enter into a trance state.

---

1   The third heaven could be equated with paradise, and the two terms are interchangeable. "Third heaven. It is quite useless to attempt to explain this expression according to any scheme of celestial gradation. The conception of seven heavens was familiar to the Jews; but according to some of the Rabbis there were two heavens—the visible clouds and the sky; in which case the third heaven would be the invisible region beyond the sky. Some think that Paul describes two stages of his rapture; the first to the third heaven, from which he was borne, as if from a halting-point, up into Paradise." (Cited from Vincent, M. R. (1887). Word studies in the New Testament. New York: Charles Scribner's Sons (public domain)).

The Damascus Road vision was one of a number of times when God revealed things to Paul. During none of these was Paul in a trance of the kind understood in shamanistic settings.

JOSEPH, HUSBAND OF MARY

On four occasions an angel appeared to Joseph in a dream. These are all in Matthew's Gospel, 1:20; 2:13; 2:19; 2:22. A dream occurs while asleep, and both sleeping and dreaming are a part of the normal human experience. God's speaking to people in this way is not uncommon in Scripture.

Joseph made no attempt to receive communication via a dream, and there is no mention of an altered state of consciousness. Nowhere in Scripture do people practice hearing from God by dreams. Modern missionaries report that Muslims, in particular, have dreamt of Jesus Christ and considered such to be a direct means of communication with them. Though this is not a common or normal part of the Christian life, it is definitely far different from shamanistic experiences.

JOHN

John the apostle was the author of the Gospel of John, the three letters of 1st, 2nd, and 3rd John, and also of Revelation, the last book in the New Testament. He wrote the following introductory remarks for Revelation:

> I, John, your brother and partner in the tribulation and the kingdom and the patient endurance that are in Jesus, was on the island called Patmos on account of the word of God and the testimony of Jesus. I was in the Spirit on the Lord's day, and I heard behind me a loud voice like a trumpet saying, "Write what you see in a book and send it to the seven churches, to Ephesus and to Smyrna, and to Pergamum and to Thyatira and to Sardis and to Philadelphia and to Laodicea" (Revelation 1:9-11).

By the last decade of the first century A.D., John was the only surviving member of the Twelve apostles called out and appointed by Jesus. He was pastor of the Church at Ephesus, and many scholars think he acted as a bishop or superintendant of a number of churches in what is now Turkey but was then designated Asia by the Romans.

Due to reasons unstated, the Romans had exiled John to Patmos during the last decade of the first century.[2] A small island in the Aegean Sea off the west coast of Turkey, Patmos served as a prison, much like the French used Devil's Island.

On a Sunday, called the Lord's Day by Christians of the time, he was "in the Spirit."[3]

Does "in the Spirit" mean that John was in some sort of trance? There are three other places in Revelation where we find a phrase similar to "in the Spirit." The first is in 4:2: "At once I was in the Spirit;" the second is in 17:3: "he carried me away in the Spirit into a wilderness," and the third in 21:10: "he carried me away in the Spirit to a great, high mountain." In Matthew 22:43 is also the same phrase, "in the Spirit," used in reference to King David, the Psalmist, when he wrote Psalm 110:1.

"In the Spirit" is a code phrase used by Jewish and other writers in the literary genre we know as apocalyptic. "In the Spirit" is an expression used to indicate inspiration; it was a way of signaling a communication from God. It is the language of the prophet, a way of saying, "These are not my words, but they are words from the Lord." The prophet Ezekiel would be

---

2   The date, although unknown, is thought to be about A.D. 96. Some scholars think the Apostle John did not write the book but that, due to differences in literary style, a John the Elder did. Some think an assistant or secretary acted as amanuensis for John or took on his mantle, due to the similarity of themes with the Gospel of John. Most, however, believe the source to be John himself.

3   A primary reason the early Christians worshipped on Sunday rather than on the Jewish Sabbath was due to Jesus' resurrection on a Sunday.

the prime example of such usage. John, and Ezekiel centuries earlier, wrote during times when the Holy Spirit of God was directly present and speaking to the prophet. In this manner, Jesus' entire ministry could be referred to as being "in the Spirit." This is a far cry, however, from the trance state. Those Bible personages who were "in the Spirit" did not prepare to enter into a state of trance.

SUMMARY STATEMENT

From Jacob to John, the Triune God – Father, Son, and Holy Spirit –interacted with kings, prophets, and apostles. While these interactions are rather mysterious, and we lack clear information as to their exact nature, the biblical spiritual experiences are nothing like the deliberate trance inducement discussed throughout this book. The differences are qualitatively distinct.

SARAH YOUNG: "JESUS CALLING"

S arah Young, as mentioned earlier, practices "listening prayer," in which she hears messages directly communicated from Jesus.

She describes her technique in her bestselling book, *Jesus Calling*, which has sold over nine million copies in twenty-six languages (as of the end of 2013). This book was the fifth bestseller for the first half of 2013 for all books, not just Christian books. Through it all, the author maintains a low profile, partly due to physical disabilities, and thus she is relatively unknown. She has experienced chronic physical difficulties for many years and writes inspiringly of her loving connection with whom or what she thinks is Jesus giving her comforting and encouraging messages.

It all began with Sarah wondering if she could receive messages during times of prayer. She hoped God would talk to her personally. And it began to happen. And yes, she believes that Jesus is really and actually speaking with her. She prays then listens, and He answers. This has been her experience for many years.

As she hears, Sarah journals what she hears, and after a number of years she published some of what she heard. Readers and prayer groups are encouraged and comforted by the messages, and as sales of books demonstrate, she has a growing audience. Many thousands are now taking up the practice of listening prayer.

The key question which must be asked is, who is speaking? Jesus or someone else? Is it possible there is clever counterfeiting here?

Over the centuries Christians have thought that God does speak to them. Richard Foster, who champions contemplative prayer or meditative prayer, defends Young's practice. He has modeled his own recommendations for deep meditation and contemplation on what Teresa of Avila, St. John of the Cross, Ignatius Loyola, and many others practiced and experienced centuries ago. What Young does is the same as or quite similar to the exercises of these Christian mystics.

Sarah Young describes her own custom as meditating on Scripture and then waiting quietly to hear a reply from Jesus. When Jesus speaks she writes down what she heard or was placed on her heart. She insists that the words or messages are not revelatory in the sense of prophecy or fortune telling; the content of the messages is fairly ordinary and biblically based. The Bible plays a major role in Sarah's life, and she firmly believes it is the inspired revelation of God; however, and this is a huge "however," she wanted more than what the Bible offers. She indeed got more and has come to rely on these communications, the "encouraging directives from the Creator," as she likes to say.

But there is a worrisome twist. When Young journals the words supposedly spoken by Jesus they are written in the first person with Jesus as the person speaking. She does not, for instance, write, "Jesus said," but rather, "Focus on me." Since she purports to write down whatever Jesus says, her readers must logically conclude that her journal is as authoritative as the Bible, almost a fifth Gospel. If this is not so, then *Jesus Calling* is pseudo-biblical, an imitation, albeit very clever, of a revelation from God.

Young's error is therefore serious and similar to that of the Course in Miracles, supposedly communicated by Jesus to Helen Schucman in the 1970s. Schucman's Jesus dictated profoundly spiritual concepts to her, which she wrote down, and one of the most successful new age cults was born. Schucman's Jesus bears little resemblance to the biblical Jesus, unlike Young's Jesus, but could this make the counterfeit even more difficult to detect?

Young's book sales are phenomenal, and again I cannot help but be reminded of Helen Schucman and the Course in Miracles; however, Young's book is far more biblically Christian than Schucman's. The difference seems clear, and I am tempted to embrace Young's claim to hear the voice of Jesus. But it will not work. There is neither biblical precedent nor warrant for quieting oneself, praying, and then listening for Jesus to speak. Young's techniques fit into the broad spectrum that is Charisma today, emboldening yet another dangerous counterfeit practice.

The Jesus supposedly speaking to Sarah Young is very affirming and encouraging, but little else. The messages lack the doctrinal content of the real Jesus found in Scripture. Encouraging promises found in quotes supposedly from Jesus appeal to those who are easily dazzled by assurances of personal satisfaction and are therefore attracted to purveyors of the health, wealth, and prosperity gospel.

Nowhere in Scripture does God promise to speak individually to believers or answer prayer by speaking directly to the one praying. This is the critical point. What I discovered in my decades of ministry is that, if you want to hear things from God, you eventually will hear something. But the communication is not from God, however real and spiritual the communication might be.

John 10:27 is quoted by proponents of Young's book as proof that Jesus speaks directly to His '"sheep." "My sheep hear my voice, and I know them, and they follow me." To "hear" is to know Jesus as the Good Shepherd as distinct from a false shepherd or a wolf; the literal application of "hear" does not work here. It is the Holy Spirit who indwells the believer at conversion who "bears witness with our spirit that we are children of God" (Romans 8:16).

An instruction for believers to listen for the actual audible voice of Jesus is foreign to the New Testament writings. There is nothing in Scripture about praying then listening for a response. It is surprising that so many do not know this. Churches across the country have instituted prayer groups devoted to Young's methods. Again, it illustrates the fascination with feelings and direct experiences rather than seeking to learn what the Word of God actually teaches.

We are all hungry to know more of God, and little by little we do grow up into the fullness of the stature of Christ (see Ephesians 4:1-16). Following Jesus is a lifelong process and there are no short cuts. Quick and easy methods of "going direct" to the source can be addictive and difficult to disengage from. Christians are yet sinners and living in a sinful world; we are pilgrims traveling the straight and narrow road that is often filled with pain and sorrow. God hears our prayers and does strengthen and comfort us, but He speaks to us through the Scripture. That is enough for us. We do not need more. Eve wanted more and she got it, but it brought disaster upon her and all of us.

THE "THIRD HEAVEN"

P aul once said he went to the third heaven:

I must go on boasting. Though there is nothing to be gained by it, I will go on to visions and revelations of the Lord. I know a man in Christ who fourteen years ago was caught up to the third heaven—whether in the body or out of the body I do not know, God knows. And I know that this man was caught up into paradise— whether in the body or out of the body I do not know, God knows— and he heard things that cannot be told, which man may not utter. On behalf of this man I will boast, but on my own behalf I will not boast, except of my weaknesses (1 Corinthians 12:1-5).

PAUL'S VISIONS

Most commentators think 2 Corinthians was written in A.D. 55-57, so this vision occurred fourteen years earlier, around the time of his second visit to Jerusalem and before his first missionary journey. His third heaven experience would have been, it is speculated, his third vision. A record of Paul's visions is as follows: (1) on the day of his conversion he had a vision of the glorified Christ – Acts 9:3 and 22:6; (2) a vision of Ananias coming to him – Acts 9:12; (3) a vision showing he would minister to Gentiles – Acts 22:17; (4) his vision-call to Macedonia – Acts 16:9; (5) an encouraging vision when difficulty arose in Corinth – Acts 18:9-10; (6) a vision that followed his arrest in Jerusalem – Acts 23:11; (7) a vision during a storm at sea – Acts 27:23; and (8) a vision that gave him insight into understanding the mysteries of Christ – Ephesians 3: 1-6.[1]

It is likely that the report of Paul's vision revealed in 2 Corinthians was the first time he mentioned it. He likely did so because some detractors who had come into the Corinthian church were challenging his status as an authentic apostle, thereby attempting to downgrade the doctrines and theologies Paul preached. Paul's critics elevated themselves by claiming supernatural knowledge obtained by means of dreams and visions. For millennia shamans had gained authority by claiming direct encounters with supernatural entities, and this tradition was alive and well in the Graeco-Roman world. It is alive and well in our own day, and shamans continue to enter into a trance state, a soul journey to heaven or hell, in order to bring back information to a client, information the client would be glad to hear.

Reluctantly, Paul describes a vision he had, in order to assert his status and authority as a true apostle of Christ. He does not employ typical shamanistic language, however, nor does he use such trance-inducing techniques such as meditation, mind-altering substances, dancing, physical deprivations, or any magical devices.

PAUL'S LIMITATIONS

Paul had not known Jesus during the days of the Lord's earthly ministry. The apostles in Jerusalem and the general Christian community had been afraid of Paul, because they knew well enough of his career as their persecutor when he was named Saul. Paul had little chance yet to establish himself, whether by personal testimony or through second hand

---

1   It has been suggested that this last vision as mentioned in Ephesians 3 is a reference to the same vision spoken of in our passage in 2 Corinthians. I will not commit either way.

accounts of his dramatic reformation. Being zealous for the work of Christ and for the well being of the churches that he founded, he wrote of what he could, though at the stage in his career in A.D. 55-57, the Corinthians would have had little information to confirm Paul as a full-fledged messenger of the Gospel. But Paul had been to the third heaven.

A COMMONSENSE VIEW

Jewish people generally thought the first heaven consisted of the clouds and the air that humans breathed. The second heaven held the lights above the clouds – the sun, moon, and stars. The third heaven was where God dwelt – His abode.[2] The foregoing is a generalized way that Jewish people conceived of what was above them. God was above them, far away, and transcendent over them yet with them at the same time.

Paradise was considered the same as the third heaven. Paradise is a loan word from the Persians meaning "garden" and was a reference to the garden where God walked and talked with Adam and Eve. Fellowship restored with the Creator would take place in Paradise, the dwelling place of God.

CAUGHT UP

Paul had been "caught up to the third heaven," surely a way of describing the real presence of the transcendent God. He humbly refers to himself in the third person, and he did not know whether he was in the body or out of the body. Not too much should be made of Paul's inability or refusal to be more concrete. The distance between his experience and mechanisms used by shamans for vision questing is very great.

Despite the other visions to which Paul referred (see

---

2   Some Jewish traditions report seven heavens, even ten. The use of numbers like three, seven, and ten have special meaning in ancient Jewish beliefs, as well as in Scripture, and point to completeness, wholeness, and fulfillment. "Third heaven": surely the very presence of God.

above), this is the only time he reports being in the presence of God, or in the third heaven. My opinion is that Paul's vision and revelation would be like other visions reported in the New Testament. For instance, John was "in the Spirit" on the Lord's day when he received what we know as Revelation, the last book of the New Testament (see Revelation 1:9-11). What "in the Spirit" means is uncertain, and it may or may not be the same as a vision.

Paul's experience simply happened to him; he did not seek it. It came upon him in much the same way as what happened to John on Patmos. There was no "soul journey" and no mediumistic trance, nor was there a paganistic transportation facilitated by spirit guides. Without warning or expectation, Paul was suddenly seeing that which he would not speak of, even if he were able. Only God knew how it all took place, which Paul emphatically asserts with the double denial, "whether in the body or out of the body I do not know, God knows."

"He heard things that cannot be told, which man may not utter," is one of the more puzzling statements Paul makes as he describes the vision experience. Commonly, commentators suggest four different solutions to explain Paul's meaning. One, he was warned not to speak of what he had seen. Two, he could not find words suitable to describe the incredible content of the vision. Three, it would cause harm if he did so. Four, to reveal the sum and substance of the vision would make him sound like he had lost his mind. Whatever the meaning, Paul never revealed any content other than the fact of his vision.

KAT KERR AND "REVEALING HEAVEN": AN EYEWITNESS ACCOUNT

Kat Kerr, a sixty-year-old woman living in Florida (and sporting pinkish hair she insists is dyed "in obedience" to God's command), wrote the above entitled book. In it she reports not on visions but upon her direct encounters, her visits and conversations with "the Father" in heaven's "throne room."

Kerr is radically different from Paul, in that she freely talks about what she sees and hears. There is no hesitancy on her part, unlike Paul. It is apparent that her mission is to communicate what she has experienced in her visits to the "throne room."[3]

On one occasion the Father escorted her via time travel to the very event of Jesus' crucifixion. She says she was right there at the cross of Calvary. Not only that, she was there at the resurrection. Not even the shamans have been as brazen as that!

JUST LIKE THE MEDIUMS

As with the psychics and mediums of the occult branch of spiritism, Kerr "visits" deceased loved ones, in order to bring back reports to the bereaved on their status in heaven. Always she reports that the departed are securely saved and well, much to the comfort of the bereaved. In one instance, according to her testimony, a person who lost a loved one was surprised to hear of that person being in heaven at all!

She reports that every human being has at least one guardian angel from the moment of conception. These angels go with the believer along the road of life, helping and rescuing, and at death accompany them all the way to heaven. She learned that if a person had done bad things while on earth the guardian angel is owed an apology upon arrival in heaven. Sometimes, however, Jesus personally does the work of escorting to heaven, at least for those who have been especially faithful.

Some of what Kerr preaches is biblically sound and presents a standard gospel message, which is firmly in the Arminian stream. She recounts her own conversion experience at age four, then again at age five, when she prayed the sinner's prayer again just to be sure.[4] She is of a Pentecostal persua-

---

3   Ms. Kerr has recorded a number of videos and has uploaded them on YouTube. In the videos she reports on her visits, not visions, to heaven.
4   There is a mystery to conversion, and most mature Christians are

sion, and her rapidly growing audience is primarily among Charismatics and Pentecostals.

A MORE SIGNIFICANT CONCERN

It is not necessary to continue detailing the incredible things Kerr reports about her frequent visits to heaven; these can be garnered by visiting YouTube. There are other more significant and dangerous aspects to her ministry.

One, it is a divisive ministry. One either accepts what she says as true or one disagrees and objects. In the latter circumstance it is tantamount to declaring her a false prophet. The Old Testament penalty for false prophecy is stoning; the New Testament settles for simply rejecting the message. As the issue of Kerr's veracity and authenticity is forced into discussion, it will impact congregations and relationships. In some instances husbands and wives will be divided; in others, the leadership of a church may embrace Kerr while others are duty bound to reject the whole business. This is happening right now, since Kerr has caught on in a big way.

Two, acceptance of her ministry opens the door to further connection with spiritism and shamanism, for this is essentially what Kerr is up to. We do not find mention in the New Testament of congregations developing such connections or recommending them. Nowhere in Scripture are the exceptional experiences of Paul and John the same as Kerr's.

Three, there is a mind-bending process going on. Much of what she details of her visits crosses the line of what is plausible. If one accepts that Kerr visits heaven, then one is compelled to believe what she reports to happen there despite its unusual nature. With the wide acclaim Kerr is presently enjoying, people will have to suspend skepticism in order to go

aware of false conversion, especially in a culture that is saturated with Christianity. In my book, *Are You Really Born Again?: Understanding True and False Conversion*, published concurrently by Earthen Vessel Publishing and Evangelical Press, the issues of false conversion are examined.

along with the crowd. Thus comes into play the toxic or cultic mindset. Little by little we can be led astray.

Four, Kerr has a not-so-subtle expectation that others should be or could be doing what she herself is doing: you, too, can visit heaven and talk with the Father, and here's how, so why don't you? Pretty soon Christians are being moved down the "slippery slope" into the occult realm.

Five, those who are critical in their analysis are likely to be ignored or shunned if they suggest that opposing Kerr is blasphemy of the Holy Spirit or rejection of what God is doing in "these last days."

THE CORE CONTRAST BETWEEN PAUL AND KAT KERR

Paul does not state that he spoke with God – not the Father, not the Son, not the Holy Spirit – in any mention of a vision he experienced. Kat Kerr, on the other hand, does. Herein is the great contrast between Paul and Kerr, and nothing could be more telling. Kerr's picture of the Father is more akin to a description of a conversation with a human friend. I think that this is exactly what Kerr intends to convey – that she has such an exalted status that she is able to be in the very presence of God and talk directly with Him just as Adam and Eve spoke with the Creator God in the Garden of Eden before the Fall (see Genesis 2:15-17, 3:1-19).

But Paul spoke of God's utter transcendence: "He who is the blessed and only Sovereign, the King of kings and Lord of lords, who alone has immortality, who dwells in unapproachable light, whom no one has ever seen or can see" (1 Timothy 6:15b-16).

It is true that the Spirit indwells all born again Christians and, through Christ, they have access to the Father in prayer. Scripture also affirms that we rest in the finished work of Christ and cease from our efforts of trying to save ourselves. But it does not mean we may be bodily present in the heavenly places. Kerr ignores this standard and historical Christian understanding and claims to have actually been repeatedly in the very presence of God, where God dwells in "unapproachable light," as though she were nearly his equal. This contrast cannot be ignored or accepted.

IN THE LINE OF FALSE PROPHETS

Kat Kerr is not the first one to claim conscious contact with heavenly beings. One thinks of Mohammad, Joseph Smith, David Berg of the Children of God, Sun Myung Moon, and countless others. The claiming of special revelation is standard fare in the spiritual market place.

And where will this all lead regarding Kat Kerr? Her reporting is firm and clear, so there are only two responses: she is either spot on or a false prophet. She will attract a following, and churches and individuals will be forced into either compliance and acceptance or resistance and rejection of her claims.

Kat Kerr is not the only one presently claiming heavenly conversations with angels, Jesus, and the Father. Recent history shows a trend in this direction, particularly among the Fourth or Fifth Wave proponents and those who are involved with the exhibitions at the Bethel Church in Redding under the leadership of Bill Johnson. Followers of Kerr, Johnson, and others of this ilk are developing cultic expressions within the visible Christian church.

It is with a saddened heart that I write this. It is crucial, however, for Bible based Christians to stand up and be counted. Fortunately, I no longer identify with the Charismatic and Pentecostal movement, because if I did it would be harder for me to objectively analyze it.

We must recognize that not everyone who claims spiritual experiences has to be accepted and believed. False signs and wonders are performed by the power of Satan. This we know about, and the demonic tricks and deceptive attacks sometimes come from within the Christian community.

"Watch and pray," Jesus told His disciples that last night in

Gethsemane. "Beloved, do not believe every spirit, but test the spirits, whether they are of God; because many false prophets have gone out into the world" (1 John 4:1).

THE
BOTTOM LINE

Underneath Santería, Lucumi, Candomblé, Macumba, Voodoo, shamanism, Wicca, and contemporary neo-pagan spiritualities, including those spiritualities found among some Christians, is a bottom blood-red line, yet little about it is known or admitted.

Let me be blunt. The question is, who, or rather what, is being worshipped, sacrificed to, appealed to for power and knowledge, or connected with in trance states or ecstasy?

The answer is found in the Hebrew and Greek bibles, the Old and New Testaments. We first find in the Torah, the Book of Deuteronomy, chapter 32, verse 17, "They sacrificed to demons that were no gods."

This short sentence is part of the Song of Moses where Moses was speaking of the Hebrew people who were worshipping pagan gods. In Egypt, the Hebrew slaves began to take up the deities common to the Egyptians, and when things went awry on their journey to their Promised Land, they fell back into a worship of gods that were no gods.

Then is written in the New Testament in the first letter of Paul to the Corinthian church, chapter 10, verse 20, "What pagans sacrifice they offer to demons and not to God."

Corinth was a center of pagan worship where the pantheon of gods and goddesses was enjoying a revival, with shrines and temples everywhere. The mythical Greek deities, now joined with the Roman myths, captivated the minds and devotions of the common people. Paul, highly aware of the nature of this form of spirituality, did not refrain from speaking the truth.

The bottom line, largely obscured in contemporary times, must be clarified in our own period of history. A lack of critical analysis has enabled people to engage in forms of worship they would not embrace, if the reality of that worship were exposed. In a word, that reality is demonic.

Exposing this demonic foundation that supports the temples of shamanism, Santeria, Wicca, and some variant forms in what we know as charisma is the reason for the writing of this book.

GLOSSARY

TERM	DEFINITION
adura	A *Yoruba* word for prayer; a prayer that is usually directed toward a particular *orisha*.
Ark of the Covenant	From the Hebrew Bible. The ark or chest that contained the stone tablets on which the Ten Commandments were inscribed and which was placed in the Holy of Holies, the inner sanctum in the Temple.
ambient energies	Spiritual entities that happen to be nearby and to which an unsuspecting person might be susceptible. These energies are said to be potentially present in any "spirit" work, whether led by a *shaman, santero*(a), or *Wiccan* priest or priestess.
animal helpers	*Power animals.* They are sources of power for *shamans* and *pagan* priests in the *soul journey* or in ritual and ceremony. Animals like eagles, ravens, wolves, bears, hawks, coyotes, and more, are common animal symbols used by *shamans* and *pagan* priests and may be displayed on clothing, headdresses, totems, or on walls of homes.
animism	The belief that spirits inhabit all natural components of the earth, including objects such as rocks, plants, streams, animals, mountains, valleys, and so on. This belief encompasses the idea that there is no separation between the spiritual and the physical world and that souls and/or spirits exist not only in humans, but in everything else as well. It is the foundational doctrine upon which *shamanism* is based as well as most other *pagan* and *neo-pagan* religions.
apostle	From the Greek verb for "to send" – an apostle is one who is sent on a mission. The Twelve, those directly

TERM	DEFINITION
apostle (cont.)	called and commissioned by Jesus to be carriers of His message, were know as apostles. The word "missionary," derived from Latin, carries the same concept.
ASC	Altered State of Consciousness. Terms that serve as synonyms are: the *trance* state, *ecstasy*, passive state of mind, *shamanic state of consciousness (SSC)*, and others. It is a condition in which the mind is not functioning in a manner consistent with that of an ordinary waking consciousness. Some distinguish between a light, medium, and heavy state of consciousness. Attaining to an ASC may involved the use of substances like tobacco juice, *ayahuasca* (and other hallucinogenic drugs like LSD and peyote), music, dancing, chanting, singing, and these in combination. In this state the person can 'travel' to heaven or to hell and contact spirits, souls of the dead, gods and goddesses, and more.
ashé	The all powerful force or energy in *Santería*, as well as the supreme being in a non-corporeal state. Ashe is divine power that may be applied or used in a manner directed by the *shaman*. Ashe is obtained by worship and sacrifice to the *orishas*.
ashe orunmila	A sacred powder, prepared by the *babalawo*, in order to work magical rites.
asiento	A ceremony in which the initiate publically dedicates him- or herself to an *orisha*. It is spiritually analogous to a wedding ceremony. The initiate is "crowned" with the *orisha*; the *orisha* comes to live in the actual head of the initiate, constituting a possession.
astral travel	Otherwise known as Astral Projection and is also the same or similar to the concept of the *soul journey*. The experience of the soul leaving the body and traveling to the "astral plane." For some, the astral plane is thought to be a place that is populated by spirits, the destination of those who have died, and the place from which those being born emerge.

TERM	DEFINITION
ayahuasca	A hallucinogenic and dangerous drug used mostly by South American *shamans*, particularly in Columbia, Peru, and Ecuador, and which is meant to induce a *trance* state. It is made from the plant Banisteriopsis Caapi.
aura	A term used to describe a supposed electromagnetic field of energy that emanates from the body and that *shamans*, *Wiccans*, and other *occult* practitioners especially healers are said to be able to observe and evaluate for any number of purposes.
babalawo	The term means "father of mystery" and is the designation for the high priests of Santería, usually male, who are thought to be adept at fortune telling.
Babalu-Aye	An *orisha* worshipped in *Santería*, and is the god who governs illness.
bata(a)	A West African style of drumming and/or the drums used in the *bembe* of Santerían worship. Each bata is said to be possessed by a spirit who then speaks, energizes, or creates *trance*-like states in worshippers. The batas send messages to the *orishas* and invite them to join in the worship.
beltane	In *Wiccan* practice, it is the mid-point between the spring equinox and the summer solstice, and is celebrated on May Day.
bembe	*Bata* drumming and dancing festival ceremonies done to honor the *orishas* and invite the *orishas* to possess the dancers. Bembes may be conducted out of sight of the public, but are also made public and even become tourist attractions.
botánica	A retail store specializing in the sales of products such as oils, incense, candles, amulets, animals, and alternative or traditional health products. "*Pet Store*" is the name for a retail outlet that specializes in providing animals, from birds to all manner of mammals, for use in

TERM	DEFINITION
botánica (cont.)	sacrifices to *orishas* in order to obtain *ashé*.
Buddhism	A religion with its origins in India. Buddhism propounds achieving a state of "nirvana" by the cessation of suffering – suffering to be eliminated by the elimination of ignorance and desire.
Chango	One of the central *orishas* who is said to rule over lightning, thunder, and fire.
Candomblé	One of the terms used in Brazil for *Santería*. Candomblé will vary in certain details from, for instance, the *Lucumi* form of *Santería* as practiced in Cuba, and the *Voodoo* found in Haiti. The names will change from place to place, but it is still the West African worship of the *orishas*.
charisma	A term, when interpreted in the Christian sense, is related to receiving and expressing the gifts of the *Holy Spirit*. It can also refer to the general community of those who believe in the same. However, its interpretation by *Wiccans* and *Santeríans* includes identification with *altered states of consciousness* and the mechanisms to achieve these states, *trance* or *ecstasy*.
charismatic	A charismatic person is one who practices or experiences gifts of the *Holy Spirit* as recorded in Romans 12 and 1 Corinthians 12. It may also refer to the actual gifts, such as speaking in tongues, miracles, healing, and prophesy.
collares	A term for the beaded necklaces or *elekes*, which are given one being initiated into the first level of *Santería*. These are thought to provide protection. *Elekes* is a word used instead of collares in some branches of *Santería*.
contemplative prayer	As used by Christians, it is a form of prayer that focuses on God with thoughts and feelings rather than verbally expressing requests or praise. In its use by *Wiccans* and

TERM	DEFINITION
contempla-tive prayer (cont.)	*Santeríans, altered states of consciousness* are seen as prerequisites for engaging in such prayer.
cosmic tree	A *shaman* and/or *Wiccan* term for "*world tree.*" The tree symbolizes the universe in continual regeneration and represents the idea of immortality. The roots of the tree represent the *underworld*, or hell; the trunk represents the present world or reality; the leaves and upper branches represent heaven or the Wiccan *Summerland*.
coven	The group of associated *witches* that meets to celebrate *sabbats*, *esbats*, and other ceremonial rituals.
cowrie shells	Cowrie shells, used as money in Africa early on, are used in *Santería* for purposes of divination or *diloggun*. The priest, priestess, or *babalawo* casts sixteen cowrie shells out of a total of twenty-one on a special mat then interprets them along traditional guidelines.
derecho	The fee charged by *Santerían* priests and priestesses for performing rites and rituals, such as initiations, and to solve various problems, especially as related to healings. Fees for ordinations have been known to be $5,000, and in some cases, as much as $45,000.
diloggun	A system of fortune telling or divination using *cowrie shells*. The *diloggun* at one point was the sole province of the *babalawo*, but is now also performed by *santeros* and *santeras*.
divination	A ritual or process, the intent of which is to gain insight into a particular situation. It involves the reading of signs and omens and is usually intended to provide guidance as to how one should proceed.
divination Journey	Another term for a *soul journey*, used mainly in *neo-paganism* like *Wicca*, where in a state of *trance*, the practitioner goes on a spiritual trip to find information from the dead or any number of spiritual entities.

TERM	DEFINITION
drumming circle	Found among *neo-pagans* and even some charismatics, who use music, especially the drum and drumming, in order to enter into an *ecstasy* or *altered state of conscious*. For the *charismatic*, the beat of the drum helps attain what is thought of as a more 'spiritual' state.
dueño de la cabeza	A Spanish phrase meaning, "the owner of the head" and refers to the *orisha* who possesses the head, and therefore the person, of the *iyawo* or initiate.
ebbo	A ritual whereby food is offered or sacrificed to an *orisha* in order to obtain *ashé*.
ecstasy	This term is synonymous with *trance* state, *passive state of consciousness*, and *altered state of consciousness* and is a state of mind beyond a normal, waking, or ordinary state of consciousness. *Ecstasy* carries the idea of being outside oneself.
egun	Spirits of the dead, mainly one's departed ancestors.
egungun	This is a person who is possessed by an *eggun*.
elekes	See *collares*.
eleda	A guardian angel, or sometimes an *orisha* or *egun*, that inhabits or dwells in the head of and protects the *iyawo*.
eleggua	An *orisha* who serves as a messenger, "opener of the ways," a trickster, or *warrior*.
elemental powers	The four major powers, which can be summoned and employed to make *magick* work. They are: air, fire, water, and earth.
emerging church movement	A recent movement within Christian churches that attempts to 'contextualize' in order to be relevant to those who are not acquainted with Christianity or who have rejected traditional Christianity. The basic presumption is that the Church must adapt to the changes that are occurring in the culture.

TERM	DEFINITION
esbats	These are days when *Wiccans* celebrate the goddess, who is represented by the moon. There are 13 esbats every year: times when the moon is full and the goddesses power and energy are at their peak.
Espiritismo	Otherwise known as *Kardecian spiritism*. It is the belief that the dead live on and may be contacted. At the heart of Espiritismo is the *séance*, the medium, and the fortune teller. *Santería* incorporated or enfolded Espiritismo into its religion during the 19th century.
ewe	Ewe refers to herbs, plants, flowers, roots, and trees that are used as offerings to the *orishas*.
familiar spirit	A spirit that masks itself as a known person, e.g., a deceased person who is apparently contacted by a medium or channelor. The term can also have a broader meaning and may refer to a usual helper or *spirit guide*.
Florida water	A liquid with magical properties made from herbs, very favored among *Santeríans*.
Gaia	Gaia is Mother Earth, a primary if not the single central goddess in *Wiccan* and other *neo-pagan* religions. She is often summoned to participate in rites and rituals in order to obtain her *magick*.
grimoire	A witch's recipe book or list of angels, spirits, or the *magickal* properties of objects found in nature.
guardians of the watchtower	Spirits alleged to be on the same level as the Christian archangels – Gabriel, Michael, Uriel, and Raphael.
guerreros	*Warrior orishas*, namely, Eleggua, Oggun, Ochosi, and Osun, who are received by *Santeríans* for protection.
healing plants	Much the same as the *Santeríian Ewe*, plants that have either real or supposed spiritual healing properties that are used in rites and rituals by *neo-pagans*.

TERM	DEFINITION
Hinduism	A religion originating in northern India. Its core beliefs revolve around *reincarnation, karma,* and *yoga,* which is the sought after union with the supreme deity.
Holy Spirit	Especially when capitalized, this term denotes the Spirit of God, one of the three members of the Trinity as understood in Christianity.
ifa	The name of the *orisha* of the oracle -- the centerpiece of *Santerían* fortune telling. Traditionally, only the *babalawo* used a system of fortune telling known as ifa, the highest and most respected form of divination.
ilé	The *Santerían* 'church' household; a unit of the *Santerían* community. A *santero* or *santera* is the center of the ilé. Members of the ilé traditionally look to their priest or priestess for guidance and counsel.
incubus	A 'male' spirit that engages in sexual activity with a human being.
in the Spirit	An idiom found in Scripture indicating the speaker had been in the act of worshipping, praising, and praying to God. John said he was "in the Spirit on the Lord's day" (Revelation 1:10), when he received his "revelation" that we know as the Book of Revelation.
iyawo	The iyawo is the "Bride of an *orisha*." This is what the *iyawo* becomes after the initiation process (the *asiento*), when he or she is "mounted" or possessed by the *orisha* chosen for the initiate by way of fortune telling, or the *diloggun*.
Kabbalah	A set of esoteric teachings, the aim of which is to explain the relationship between God and His creation. Kabbalah is a mystical and occult-oriented offshoot of Judaism.
Kardecian spiritism	The art and practice of contacting the dead through the *séance*. Also see *Espiritismo* above.

TERM	DEFINITION
karma	In Buddhism: an action, seen as bringing upon oneself inevitable results, good or bad, either in this life or in a *reincarnation*. In *Hinduism*: one of the means of reaching Brahman. In Theosophy: the cosmic principle according to which each person is rewarded or punished in one incarnation according to that person's deeds in the previous incarnation.
kirtan	The chanting of hymns or mantras to the accompaniment of instruments (drums in particular), in forms of *Hinduism*, especially Hare Krishna.
Koan	A riddle without a solution. When focused on the koan, the mind may be shifted to a state of passivity, all designed to move one into a *trance* state.
lower world	The *underworld*, hell -- the roots part of the *Cosmic Tree*. *Power animals* can be found in journeys to the lower world.
Lucumi	The Cuban term for *Santería* and is derived from the *Yoruba* language.
Macumba	One of the Brazilian terms for *Santería*. See also *Candomblé* above.
madrina	A female leader, a god mother, within the *Santería* organization, also known as a *santera*.
magick	Magicians do magic; *Wiccans* do magick.
mantra	A phrase, word, or sound that is repeated during meditation or prayer. Can be used, in extensive repetition, to produce a *trance* state.
meditation	The act of focusing deeply on a single object, thought, or word(s). In a light sense, it is simply concentration, reflection, and rumination. However, it may also be an act of inducing one's mind to enter an altered state of consciousness by emptying it and attempting to maintain thoughtlessness .

TERM	DEFINITION
medium	A person who claims spiritual powers to contact the dead, who then receive messages from the dead or allows the dead to speak through them. In the *Santerían* bembe, the specially trained dancers, after they enter into a trance state and are therefore possessed by an orisha, proceed then to tell fortunes and perform various forms of magic.
mystic	A person who seeks by various means such as prayer, meditation, chanting, centering, concentration, achieving an *altered state of consciousness*, and more, to connect with or contact spiritual entities. The mystic enters into a *trance* state in order to attain a close or direct experience of God, goddess, or ultimate reality.
mysticism	A philosophy based on the belief that ultimate spiritual truths can be obtained while in *altered states of consciousness*. Of particular importance is the transcendental consciousness.
neo-paganism	Also known as modern *paganism* or contemporary *paganism*. Neo-paganism is an umbrella term for a religion or methodology that is based upon beliefs related to *animism* and *mysticism*. *Santeríans, shamans,* and *Wiccans* will fit into the category of neo-pagan.
Obatalá	In the *Yoruba* pantheon of thousands, Obatalá is the chief deity and creator of humanity.
occultism	Occultism is the study of occult practices, including (but not limited to) magic, alchemy, extra-sensory perception, astrology, spiritualism, and divination. Interpretation of occultism and its concepts can be found in the belief structures of philosophies and religions such as Gnosticism, Hermeticism, Theosophy, *Wicca*, Thelema, Satanism, and *neo-paganism*.
Olodumare	The name given to the one supreme *orisha* of *Santería*, the creator of all that exists. All things are believed to come from him and all things are to return to him.

TERM	DEFINITION
Olofi	When the West African slaves came to the New World, they disguised worship of the *orishas* by giving them Christian names. Olofi became Jesus. Therefore, the *Santerían* who appears to be worshipping Jesus is really worshipping Olofi.
Olosi	This is the *Santerían* term for the devil, which has to do with *Palo Mayombe* particularly.
Ooni	The spiritual head and authority over the *Yoruba* of Nigeria and all of *Santería* in the New World.
ordination	The process of learning, ritual, and ceremony that results in the acceptance and approval of an individual to hold an authoritative position, such as priest or priestness, in a religious organization.
orisha	From the *Yoruba* language of West Africa, a word used for one of thousands of gods or goddesses. Worship of them in the New World became known as *Santería*, and the number of *orishas* was reduced.
OSC	Ordinary State of Consciousness. The 'normal' state of the mind -- characterized by a beta wave state and being awake and aware. This is the very opposite of nonordinary reality, a term found among *neo-pagans*, and is another way of speaking of the *trance* or *ecstasy* states of consciousness.
otane	A stone that is said to carry within it the actual presence of an *orisha*, so that it then contains the *ashé* of the *orisha*. These stones, kept in a tureen, or deep covered dish, must be 'fed' regularly through offerings. When animals are sacrificed, the blood of the animal is to be poured or sprinkled on the stones.
padrino	The godfather, the male leader within the *Santerían ile*, and is also referred to as the *santero*.
paganism	Pagan religions (paganism) refers to a group of historical polytheistic religious traditions—primarily those of cultures known to the classical world of Greece and

TERM	DEFINITION
paganism (cont.)	Rome. In a wider sense, it has also been understood to include any non-Abrahamic, folk, or ethnic religion. It originated in the Neolithic (Stone Age) era. The term, pagan, is derived from the Latin word, paganus, which means a country dweller. The pagan usually has a belief in many gods (polytheistic), but only one is chosen as the one to worship which represents the chief god and supreme godhead.
pantheism	The belief that all that exists is in fact god. Pan, from the Latin means "all" and theism means god. Thus pantheism's deity is totally immanent and not at all transcendent.
palero	A priest of *Palo*. Also known as mayomberos.
Palo, Palo Monte, Palo Mayombe	Popular sects or subsets of *Santería* that originated in the Congo or the Bantu tribe. Palo is actually witchcraft. Palo is Spanish for branch or wooden stick, and with these the paleros do their magic. There are two types of Palo Mayombe; one has to do with the Christian God, and the other works with the devil, *Olosi*.
passive state of consciousness	A state of mind in wherein a person has deliberately gone into 'neutral' or a non-mindful and non-thoughtful state. A passive state of consciousness is equivalent to a *trance* state or *ecstasy*.
Pentecostal	"Pentecostal" describes a Christian who embraces the present day operation of the charismatic gifts of the Holy Spirit that are listed in Romans 12 and 1 Corinthians 12:4-10. Pentecostals include Protestant Christians who believe in a second experience of the Holy Spirit spoken of as "the baptism of the Holy Spirit," which is evidenced by speaking in tongues, but not always. Pentecostals are charismatic, but not all charismatics embrace a Pentecostal theology.
pet store	See *Botánica*

TERM	DEFINITION
power animal	Also *animal helper.* These are creatures encountered in the *soul journey* by the *shaman* or *Wiccan;* they assist in acquiring information and performing healings.
power object	An object thought to have magical or spiritual power that is used in ritual by *shamans* in particular but also by many *neo-pagans.*
power place	A place or spot considered to be powerful due to a concentration of power and spiritual energy and therefore may be expected to be inhabited by power spirits.
psycho-pomp	Within *shamanism*, the one who conducts souls to heaven or retrieves them from the *underworld.*
quarters	There are differences of opinion, but mainly the four directions of North, East, South and West along with the elemental powers of Earth, Air, Fire and Water comprise the quarters. All of these the *witch* may summon into the circle for help with the *magick.*
quartz crystal	Considered by *shamans* to be a *power object* and therefore useful in healings and other magical rites.
rede	The central principal of *Wicca*: "An it harm none, do what ye will."
reincarna-tion	The religious or philosophical concept that the soul or spirit, after biological death, begins a new life in a new body that may be human, animal, or spiritual depending on the moral quality of the previous life's actions. This doctrine is a central tenet of the Indian religions of *Buddhism* and *Hinduism*. It is also a common belief of various ancient and modern religions based on *spiritism* and is found in many tribal societies around the world, in places such as Siberia, West Africa, North America, and Australia.
sabbat	Sabbat is a holiday when *Wiccans* celebrate the male energy of the "All," represented by the "God" and the "Sun." There are 8 sabbats each year, and they fall on the

TERM	DEFINITION
sabbat (cont.)	equinoxes, the solstices, and the midpoints between each of these.
santera	A female leader, priestess, or *madrina* within *Santería*.
Santería	A religion originating in Africa. In Spanish, "santería" means "worship of the saints," or "that saint thing." Santería involves *mysticism*, *spiritism*, animism, and various rituals including animal sacrifice.
santero	A male leader, priest, or *madrino* within *Santería*.
shaman	One who exercises spiritual activities within the animistically-based religions founded on *shamanism*. Ethnologists and anthropologists group *witches*, witch doctors, medicine men, seers, wizards, sorcerers, holy men, and magicians with *shamanism*, with shaman becoming the catchall term for these individuals.
shamanism	A term used to apply to the underlying mystical worldview of many of the world's primitive religions. Thought to have originated in Siberia and central Asia somewhere in the Paleolithic era, thus being tens of thousands of years old. It relies upon the *shaman*, who practices his/her art of entering into a *trance* state in order to travel into the spirit world and thereby assist living clients with issues of healing and fortune telling.
shamanic journey	The trip a *shaman* or *Wiccan* takes after he or she goes into an *altered state of consciousness* or *trance* so that contact and communication can be established in the spirit world.
SSC	Shamanic State of Consciousness - See ASC.
séance	A gathering led by a medium, psychic, channelor, *shaman*, or other person considered to have contact with the *underworld* or realm of the dead, for the purpose of making contact with the spirits or souls of the deceased.

TERM	DEFINITION
soaking prayer	A mystical activity involving meditation and a *trance* state generally practiced by *charismatics* and *Pentecostals.*
solitaire	A *witch* who practices alone and is not in a *coven.*
soul	There are two fundamental definitions or understandings about "soul." The first is an ethereal or spirit (ghost) presence that has an existence separate from the body and that may have a pre-existence and/or survives the death of the body. The second sees soul as a synonym for the person and points to the spiritual nature of a human being. Because there is no separate existence, either pre or post earthly life, when the person dies there is no soul that remains.
soul journey	A journey undertaken by a *Wiccan* while in an *altered state of consciousness*. This journey is embarked upon for the purpose of healing, working *magick*, retrieving information, telling the future, or communicating with the dead.
sozo prayer	A prayer, mystical in its approach, wherein a mediator/guide encourages the subject to enter a mild *trance* and leads the subject to connect with his or her own deep feelings, the impact of which is that the subject is alleged to be experiencing contact with the *Holy Spirit*. Sozo Prayer, like *soaking prayer,* is mostly found among *charismatics* and *Pentecostals.*
spirit guide	See *Familiar Spirit.*
spiritism	The belief that the dead live on and can be contacted. See also *Espiritismo.*
SSC	The Shamanic State of Consciousness is a way of describing the *trance* state or *ecstasy*. See *ASC.*
succubus(ae)	Demons that assume a female human form and may have sexual intercourse with humans. See also *incubus.*

TERM	DEFINITION
Sufism	A mystically oriented religion that branched off from Sunni Islam and that uses music and dancing to achieve *altered states of consciousness.*
Summer-land	Some *witches* believe that Summerland is where spirits go after death in order to rest, reflect, and decide whether they should *reincarnate* and help future generations of *witches.*
syncretism	The merging of contradictory beliefs into a single belief system.
third heaven	Heaven is the place of the dwelling of God. In most cases this dwelling or abode of God exists outside of time and space. From ancient Jewish traditions, being in the "third heaven" would communicate being in the very presence of God. The numbers 3, 7, 10, 12, and multiples thereof are code terms indicating completion or fullness. The numbers 7 and 10 have been used much the same way as 3. So, 3, 7, and 10 – in regard to heaven or God's abode – carry the same meaning. In many ways, it was simply a literary device.
Threefold Law	The law of *Wicca* states that whatever you put out will come back to you threefold, be it good or evil.
trance	Trance state. See *Altered State of Consciousness.*
tutelary spirit	A spirit that protects and guards the *shaman* is known as a helping, *familiar*, or tutelary spirit. This spirit is said to serve the *shaman.*
under world	The roots of the *Cosmic Tree* or *World Tree*. Often indicates hell.
upper world	The heaven, that realm which is above and where the *spirit guides* and helpers may be found.
visuali-zation	The act of creating a picture in one's mind's eye of that which the magickian wants to happen.

TERM	DEFINITION
Voodoo, Voudun	The magical rites of *Santería* found in Haiti and other places where French is spoken in the Caribbean and West Africa.
warrior	An *orisha* whose function is to attack anyone who tries to do harm. See *guerreros.*
Wicca	A witchcraft religion whose origins are in England. It is an advanced form of *shamanism*. The Wiccan is a participant in Wicca.
witch	A common term for the female participant in *Wicca.*
world tree	The three parts of the World Tree are: roots, which symbolize the *underworld*; trunk, which symbolizes the middle earth and life on the earth; and branches with leaves, which symbolize the *upper world*. See *Cosmic Tree.*
Yoga	Yoga originated in ancient India. The intent of Yoga is for the participant to attain perfect peace through union with the supreme deity.
Yoruba	A tribal identity with origins in West Africa, particularly in southern Nigeria. Also the name of a religion based on the concept of *animism*.
Zen	Zen originated in China and Tibet, and is an offshoot or sect of *Buddhism*. It emphasizes attaining to enlightenment and employs passive or *altered states of consciousness* as part of that quest.

BIBLIOGRAPHY

Note: Many of the entries do not have publisher information. Prior to the presence of the internet, such data was helpful. Today the need for such has radically diminished.

SHAMANISM

Andrews, Ted. *Animal Speak: The Spiritual & Magical Powers of Creatures Great & Small,* 2002.

Cowan, Tom. *Fire in the Head: Shamanism and the Celtic Spirit,* 1993.

Deatsman, Colleen and Sandra Ingerman. *The Hollow Bone: A Field Guide to Shamanism,* 2011.

Denney, Michael William. *Shamanism for "White" People: Reclaiming our Animist Heritage,* 2012.

Dodgson, JoAnne. *Unleashing Love: Medicine Stories to Feed Your Spirit and Awaken Your Heart,* 2012

Eliade, Mircea. *Shamanism: Archaic Techniques of Ecstasy.* trans., Willard R. Trask. 2nd paperback ed. Princeton: Princeton University Press, 2004.

Ewing, Jim PathFinder. *Reike Shamanism: A Guide to Out-of-Body Healing.* Scotland: Findhorn Press, 2008.

Grim, John A. *The Shaman: Patterns of Siberian and Ojibway Healing,* 1983.

Harner, Michael. *The Way of the Shaman.* 10th anniversary ed. San Francisco: HarperCollins, 1990.

_____. *Cave and Cosmos: Shamanic Encounters with Another Reality,* 2013.

Heaven, Ross. *Plant Spirit Shamanism: Traditional Techniques for*

Healing the Soul, 2006.

Lewis, I.M. *Ecstatic Religion: An Anthropological Study of Spirit Possession and Shamanism,* 1971.

_____. *Ecstatic Religion: A Study of Shamanism and Spirit Possession,* 2003.

_____. *Ecstatic Religion: A Study of Shamanism and Spirit Possession,* 3rd edition, 2007

Ingerman, Sandra and Hank Wesselman. *Awakening to the Spirit World: The Shamanic Path of Direct Revelation,* 2010.

_____. *Soul Retrieval: Mending the Fragmented Self,* 2006.

Kaldera, Raven and Galina Krasskova. *Neolithic Shamanism: Spirit Work in the Norse Tradition,* 2012.

Mackinnon, Christa. *Shamanism and Spirituality in Therapeutic Practice: An Introduction,* 2012.

O'Neil, Ilsya. *Shamanism: A Spiritual Journey,* 2014.

Pinchbeck, Daniel. *Breaking Open the Head: A Psychedelic Journey into the Heart of Contemporary Shamanism,* 2003.

Pritchard, Evan T. *Bird Medicine: The Sacred Power of Bird Shamanism,* 2013.

Rinpoche, Tenzin and Mark Dahlby. *Healing with Form, Energy, and Light: The Five Elements in Tibetan Shamanism, Tantra, and Dzogchen,* 2002.

Rysdyk, Evelyn and Sandra Ingerman. *Spirit Walking: A Course in Shamanic Power,* 2013.

Scott, Gini Graham. *The Complete Idiot's Guide to Shamanism.* Indianapolis, IN: Alpha Books, 2002.

Sha, Lynne. *The Art of Shamanism,* 2014.

Smith, C. Michael. *Jung and Shamanism is Dialogue,* 2007

Stern, David. "Masters of Ecstasy." *National Geographic,* December, 2012. accessed online at www.ngm.nationalgeographic.com/2012/12/shamans/stern-text on 12/4/2013.

Stevens, Lena. *Secrets of Shamanism: Tapping the Spirit Power Within You,* 2014.

Taussign, Michael. *Shamanism, Colonialism, and the Wild Man: A Study in Terror and Healing,* 1991.

Vitebsky, Piers. *Shamanism,* 2001.

Walsh, Roger. *The World of Shamanism: New Views of an Ancient Tradition.* Woodbury, MN: Llewellyn Publications, 2011.

Weatherup, Katie. *Practical Shamanism, A Guide for Walking in Both Worlds*, 2006.
Winkelman, Michael. *Shamanism: A Biopsychological Paradigm of Consciousness and Healing*, 2010.

SANTERÍA

Amira, John and Steven Cornelius. *The Music of Santería: Traditional Rhythms of the Bata Drums*, 1999.
Black, S. Jason and Christopher H. Hyatt. *Urban Voodoo: A Beginners Guide to Afro-Caribbean Magic*, 2011.
Brown, David H. *Santería Enthroned: Art, Ritual, and Innovation in an Afro-Cuban Religion*, 2003.
Canizares, Raul. *Cuban Santería: Walking with the Night*. Rochester, VT: Destiny Books, 1999.
_____. *Babalu-Aye: Santería and the Lord of Pestilence*, 2000.
_____. *Obatala: Santería and the White Robed King of the Orishas*, 2000.
_____. *Ogun: Santería and the Master of Iron*, 2006.
Clark, Mary Ann. *Santería: Correcting the Myths and Uncovering the Realities of a Growing Religion*, 2007.
Cortez, Julio Garcia. *The Osha: Secrets of the Yoruba-Lucumi-Santería Religion in the United States*, 2013.
De La Torre, Miguel A. *Santería: The Beliefs and Rituals of a Growing Religion in America*. Grand Rapids, MI: William B. Eerdmans, 2004.
Ellis, A. B. *Yoruba-Speaking Peoples of the Slave Coast of West Africa*. 1894. reprint Lexington, KY: Moorthings, Inc., 2011
González-Wippler, Migene. *Santería: The Religion*. 2nd ed. Woodbury, MN: Llewellyn Publications, 2010.
_____. *Powers of the Orishas: Santería and the Worship of the Saints*, 1992.
_____. *Santería: African Magic in Latin America*, 2007.
_____. *Santería Experience*, 2008
Hagedom, Katherine J. *Divine Utterances: The Performance of Afro-Cuban Santería*, 2001
Hallen, Barry. *The Good The Bad and The Beautiful: Discourse about Values in Yoruba Culture*. Bloomington, IN: Indiana University Press, 2000.

Kail, Tony M. *A Cop's Guide to Occult Investigations: Understanding Satanism, Santería, Wicca, and other Alternative Religions,* 2003.

King, Charles Spencer. *Nature's Ancient Religion: Orisha Worship & Ifa,* 2008.

Lele, Ocha'ni. *The Diloggun: The Orishas, Proverbs, Sacrifices and Prohibitions of Cuban Santería,* 2003.

_____. *Sacrificial Ceremonies of Santería: A Complete Guide to the Rituals and Practices,* 2012.

Lopez, Christian. *Lukumi: Santería's Beliefs, Principles, and Direction in the Twenty-First Century,* 2004.

Mason, Michael Atwood. *Living Santería: Rituals and Experiences in an Afro-Cuban Religion,* 2002.

Mchawi, Kemba, *Growing up Yoruba: A Teen Guide for Practicing the Yoruba Lucumi Tradition,* 2013.

Montenegro, Carlos. *Santería Formulacy & Spellbook: Candles, Oils, and Incense,* 1998.

Olmas, Margarite Fernandez, Joseph M. Murphy, and Gebert Paravisini. *Creole Religions of the Caribbean: An Introduction from Vodou and Santería to Obeah and Espiritismo, second edition,* 2011.

Murphy, Joseph M. *Santería: African Spirits in America.* Boston: Beacon Press, 1993.

Smith, *Robert S. Kingdoms of the Yoruba, 3rd ed.* Madison, WI: The University of Wisconsin Press, 1988.

The Book of Palo, 2002. (no author given)

Velez, Maria. *Drumming For the Gods,* 2000.

Wedel, Johan. *Santería Healing: A Journey into the Afro-Cuban World of Divinities, Spirits, and Sorcerers,* 2003.

Zolrak. *Tarot of the Orishas Book,* 1990.

WICCA AND NEO-PAGAN RELIGION

Adams, W. H. Davenport. *Witch, Warlock, and Magician: Historical Sketches of Magic and Witchcraft in England and Scotland,* 2012.

Adler, Margo. *Drawing Down the Moon: Witches, Druids, Goddess-Worshippers and Other Pagans in America Today.* (Rev. and Exp.) New York: Penguin Books, 1986.

Albertson, Alaric. *To Walk a Pagan Path: Practical Spirituality for Every Day*, 2013.

Aten, James. *The Truth About Wicca and Witchcraft Finding Your True Power*, 2011.

Audrin, Alice F. *Energy Healing, Herbal Magic, Protection Charms – A Wiccan Practical Guide*, 2012.

Benson, Bridget. *Wiccan Spells for Beginners: Improve Your Wealth, Relationships, Health and More!* 2013.

Berger, Helen A. and Douglas Ezzy. *Teenage Witches: Magical Youth and the Search for the Self.* Rutgers University Press, 2007.

Berger, Helen, Evan Leach, and Leigh S. Shaffer. *Voices from the Pagan Census: A National Survey of Witches and Neo-Pagans in the United States.* Columbia, U. of South Carolina Press, 2003.

Brines, M.E. *Of Myth and Magic*, 2011.

Brooks Medicine Eagle. *The Last Ghost Dance*, 2000.

Brown, Doreen. *Wicca for Beginners: Spelling it Out!* 2011.

Buckland, Raymond. *Buckland's Complete Book of Witchcraft (Llewellyn's Practical Magick)*, 2002.

_____. *Wicca For One: The Path of Solitary Witchcraft*, 2004.

Cowan, Douglas. *Cyberhenge: Modern Pagans on the Internet*, 2005.

Cunningham, Scott. Living *Wicca: A Further Guide for the Solitary Practitioner*, 2005.

_____. *Cunningham's Encyclopedia of Magical Herbs*, 1985.

_____. *The Complete Book of Incense, Oils and Brews*, 2002.

_____. *Cunningham's Encyclopedia of Wicca in the Kitchen*, 2002.

Dean, Cate. *Rest For The Wicked – The Claire Wiche Chronicles Book 1*, 2012.

d'Este, Sorita. *Towards the Wiccan Circle – A Practical Introduction to the Principles of Wicca*, 2008.

DeWan, Jennifer and Lohan, David. *Open Secrets: An Irish Perspective on Trafficking and Witchcraft*, 2012.

Drew, A.J. *Wicca for Men*, 2000.

Dunwich, Gerina. *The Wicca Spellbook: A Witch's Collection of Wiccan Spells, Potions, and Recipes*, 2000.

Enredy, James. *Shamanism for Beginners: Walking with the World's Healers of Earth and Sky.* Woodbury, MN: Llewellyn

Publications, 2009.

Farrar, Stewart and Janet Farrar. *A Witches' Bible: The Complete Witches' Handbook,* 1996.

Gallagher, Ann-Marie. *The Wicca Bible: The Definitive Guide to Magic and the Craft,* 2005.

Gardner, Gerald B. *The Gardnerian Book of Shadows.* Forgotten Books, www.forgottenbooks.org, 2008 (1950).

_____. *Witchcraft Today.* New York: Kensington Publishing, 2004 (1954).

_____. *The Meaning of Witchcraft.* Boston: Weiser Books, 2004.

Graner, Katie. *Wiccan Spell Casting,* 2012.

Griffin, Wendy ed. *Daughters of the Goddess.* Walnut Creek, CA: AltaMira Press, 2000.

Harding, Stephan. *Animate Earth: Science, Intuition, and Gaia.* White River Junction, VT: Chelsea Green Publishing, 2006.

Holland, Eileen and Raymond Buckland. *The Wicca Handbook,* 2008.

Hutton, Ronald. *The Triumph of the Moon: A History of Modern Pagan Witchcraft.* New York: Oxford University Press, 1999.

Llewellyn. *Llewellyn's 2014 Witches' Datebook,* 2013.

_____. *Llewellyn's 2014 Magical Almanac: Practical Magic for Everyday Living,* 2013.

McLarney, Jeanne and D.J. Conway. *Wicca: The Complete Craft,* 2001.

Medicine Eagle, Brooke. *The Last Ghost Dance: A Guide for Earth Mages.* New York: Ballantine Wellspring, 2000.

Moura, Ann. *Grimoire for the Green Witch: A Complete Book of Shadows,* 2003.

Paxson, Diana L. *Trance-Portation: Learning to Navigate the Inner World.* San Francisco: Weiser Books, 2008.

Plaskow, Judith and Carol P. Christ, eds. *Weaving the Visions: New Patterns in Feminist Spirituality.* San Francisco: Harper Collins, 2000.

Proctor-Smith, Marjorie and Janet R. Walton. *Women at Worship: Interpretations of North American Diversity.* Louisville: Westminster/John Knox Press, 1993.

Rasbold, Katrine and Rasbold, Eric. *Magical Ethics and Protection,* 2013.

RavenWolf, Silver. *Solitary Witch: The Ultimate Book of Shadows for the New Generation,* 2003.

Roderick, Timothy. *Wicca: A Year and a Day: 36 of the Wise,* 2005.

Russell, Jeffrey and Brooks Alexander. *A New History of Witchcraft, Sorcerers, Heretics and Pagans.* London: Thames and Hudson, 2007.

Sabin, Thea, *Wicca for Beginners: Fundamentals of Philosphy & Practice.* Woodbury, MN: Llewellyn Publications, 2006.

Scarabeo, Lo. *Wicca Pocket Journal,* 2014.

_____. *Wicca Cards,* 2013.

Smith, Diane. *Wicca and Witchcraft For Dummies,* 2005.

Starhawk, Sky. *The Fifth Sacred Thing.* New York: Bantam Books, 1993.

Starwind, Raven. *The Ultimate Wicca Handbook,* 2012.

Walsh, Milla. *Wicca Candle Spells: Simple Magic Spells That Work Fast,* 2013.

Windsor, Lynn. *Western Winds Wicca Volume 2: Ritual Grimoire,* 2014.

Zimmerman, Denise and Katherine A. Gleason, revised with Miria Liguana. *The Complete Idiot's Guide to Wicca and Witchcraft.* 3rd edition. New York: Alpha Books, 2006.

Zoe, Frater. *The Rite of the Moon,* 2013.

Zurich, Holly. *Simple Wiccan Magick Full Moon Spells & Rituals,* 2012.

CHARISMA

Baker, Heidi. *Birthing the Miraculous: The Power of Personal Encounters with God to Change Your Life and the World,* 2014.

Bickle, Mike. *Growing in the Prophetic: A Balanced Guide to Using and Nurturing Dreams, Revelations and Spiritual Gifts.* Charisma House, 2013.

Brown, Candy Gunther. *Testing Prayer: Science and Healing,* 2012.

Brown, Michael L. *Authentic Fire,* 2014.

_____. *The Revival Answer Book,* 2001.

Cho, David Yonngi. *Prayer That Brings Revival: Interceding for God to Move in your Family, Church, and Community, 1998.*

Clark, Randy and Johnson, Bill. *There is More!: The Secret to Experiencing God's Power to Change Your Life,* 2013.

Clinton, Robin. *When God Speaks...Who Will Listen,* 2011.

Colley, Lindell. *Brownsville Worship: Volume One, Music from the Pensacola Revival,* 1999.

Dedmon, Kevin. *The Ultimate Treasure Hunt: A Guide to Supernatural Evangelism Through Supernatural Encounters,* 2007.

DeLoriea, Renee. *Portal in Pensacola: The Real Thing Hits Brownsville,* 1997.

Fortner, Michael. *The Almost True Yet False Prophet,* 2013.

Hancock, Rita. *Radical Well-being: A Biblical Guide to Overcoming Pain, Illness, and Addictions,* 2013.

Hanegraaff, Hank. *Counterfeit Revival: Looking for God in All the Wrong Places.* Thomas Nelson, 2001.

Hill, Stephen and Patrick Waters. *The Pursuit of Revival: Igniting a Passionate Hunger for More of God,* 1997.

Hill, Stephen. *The God Mockers: And Other Messages from the Brownsville Revival,* 1997.

_____. *White Cane Religion: And Other Messages from the Brownsville Revival,* 1997.

Johnson, Bill, Dick Mills, Randy Clark, and Jack Taylor. *Supernatural Power of the Transformed Mind,* 2005.

Johnson, Bill and Randy Clark. *The Essential Guide to Healing,* 2011.

Johnson, Bill and Heidi Baker. *Hosting the Presence: Unveiling Heaven's Agenda,* 2012.

Johnson, Bill and Beni Johnson. *The Happy Intercessor,* 2009.

Johnson, Bill. *When Heaven Invades Earth,* 2005.

_____. *Face to Face With God: The Ultimate Quest to Experience His Presence,* 2007.

Kendall, R.T. *Holy Fire: A Balanced, Biblical Look at the Holy Spirit's Work in Our Lives,* 2014.

Kilpatrick, John and David Yonggi Cho. *Fest of Fire: The Father's Day Outpouring,*1995.

Lane, Vann. *Children of Revival,* 1998.

Lederle, Henry. *Theology with Spirit: The Future of the Pentecostal-*

Charismatic Movements in the 21st century. Word & Spirit Press, 2010.

MacArthur, John. *Strange Fire,* 2013.

_____. *Charismatic Chaos.* Zondervan, 1993.

Menzies, Robert. *Pentecost: This Story is Our Story.* Gospel Publishing House, 2013.

Olney, Dwight J. *Sacred Sedition: Sinful Pursuit of God.* Word Alive Press, 2014.

Oropeza, B.J. *A Time to Laugh: The Holy Laughter Phenomenon Examined,* 2012.

Perry, Mark. *Kingdom Churches: New Strategies For a Revival Generation,* 2013.

Rabey, Steve. *Revival in Brownsville: Pensacola, Pentecostalism, and the Power of American Revivalism,* 1998.

Roberson, Dave. *The Walk of the Spirit – The Walk of Power: the Vital Role of Praying in Tongues,* 1999.

Ruckman, Peter S. *Modern Charismatic Revival Doctrines Examined,* 2012.

Smith, Chuck. *Charisma vs. Charismania,* 1983.

Strietzel, Lynn. *3 Days in Glory: Visiting Bethel Church Making the Most of 72 Hours,* 2012.

Strom, Andrew. *Kundalini Warning: Are False Spirits Invading the Church?* 2010.

_____. *True & False Revival: an Insider's Warning.* Revival School, 2012.

Thompson, Damian. *Waiting for Antichrist: Charisma and Apocalypse in a Pentecostal Church,* 2005.

Vallotton, Kris and Jack Hayford. *Fashioned to Reign: Empowering Women to Fulfill Their Divine Destiny,* 2013.

Vallotton, Kris and Bill Johnson. *The Supernatural Ways of Royalty: Discovering Your Rights and Privileges of being a Son or Daughter of God,* 2006.

Vallotton, Kris. *Heavy Rain: Renew the Church, Transform the World,* 2010.

_____. *Spirit Wars: Winning the Invisible Battle Against Sin and the Enemy,* 2012.

Van Vlymen, Michael R. *How to See in the Spirit: A Practical Guide on Engaging the Spirit Realm,* 2013.

Young, Sarah, *Jesus Calling.* Nashville, TN: Thomas Nelson, 2008.

_____. *Jesus Today.* Nashville, TN: Thomas Nelson, 2012.

Welchel, Tommy and Michelle Griffith. *True Stories of the Miracles of Azusa Street and Beyond: Re-live One of The Greatest Outpourings in History,* 2013.

Wolfe, Marge. *Disgracing the Glory: A Review of the Conflict Dividing the Brownsville Revival School of Ministry,* 2001.

Wood, Cathy. *The Visitation: The Brownsville Revival,* 1997.

_____. *The Visitation: Photos and Essays from the Brownsville Revival,* 2003.

Yong, Amos. *The Spirit of Creation: Modern Science and Divine Action in the Pentecostal Charismatic Imagination,* 2011.

CHRISTIAN MYSTICISM AND CONTEMPLATIVE PRAYER

Aquinas, St. Thomas. *On Prayer and the Contemplative Life,* 2012.

Borst, James. *Contemplative Prayer: A Guide for Today's Catholic,* 1993.

Bourgeault, Cynthia. *Centering Prayer and Inner Awakening,* 2004.

Clement, Olivier. *Roots of Christian Mysticism: Texts from the Patristic Era with Commentary,* 2013.

Curran, Scott. *Living in Spiritual Consciousness,* 2013.

Cutsinger, James. *Not of This World: A Treasury of Christian Mysticism (Treasures of the World's Religions),* 2003.

Dweck, Yaacob. *The Scandal of Kabbalah: Leon Modena, Jewish Mysticism, Early Modern Venice (Jews, Christians, and Muslims from the Ancient to the Modern),* 2013.

Finley, James J. *The Beginner's Guide to Contemplative Prayer,* 2002.

_____. *Merton's Palace of Nowhere,* 2003.

Foster, Richard. *Celebration of Discipline: The Path to Spiritual Growth,* 2002.

_____. *Prayer: Finding the Heart's True Home.* Zondervan, 2002.

_____. *Streams of Living Water: Celebrating the Great Traditions of*

Christian Faith, 2001.

_____. *Sanctuary of the Soul: Journey into Meditative Prayer,* 2011.

Fox, Matthew. *Christian Mystics: 365 Readings and Meditations,* 2011.

Frenette, David. *The Path of Centering Prayer: Deepening Your Experience of God,* 2012.

Inge, William Ralph. *Christian Mysticism,* 2007.

Jaoudi, Maria. *Christian Mysticism East and West: What the Masters Teach Us,* 1998.

Keating, Thomas. *Contemplative Prayer,* 2004.

_____. *The Foundations for Centering Prayer and the Christian Contemplative Life: Open Mind, Open Heart; Invitation to Love; The Mystery of Christ,* 2002.

_____. *Intimacy with God: An Introduction to Centering Prayer,* 2009.

King, Ursula. *Christian Mystics: Their Lives and Legacies Throughout the Ages,* 2001.

Kinn, James R. *Practice of Contemplation According to John of the Cross,* 2009.

Maas, Bob. *A Prayer for Today: A Collection of Contemplative Prayers,* 2013.

Mabry, John. *Growing into God: A Beginner's Guide to Christian Mysticism,* 2012.

Macquarrie, John. *Two Worlds are Ours: an Introduction to Christian Mysticism,* 2005.

McColman, Carl. *The Big Book of Christian Mysticism: The Essential Guide to Contemplative Spirituality,* 2010.

_____. *Answering the Contemplative Call: First Steps on the Mystical Path,* 2013.

McGinn, Bernard. *The Essential Writings of Christian Mysticism,* 2006.

_____. *The Foundations of Mysticism: Origins to the Fifth Century,* 2004.

_____. *The Flowering of Mysticism: Men and Women in the New Mysticism: 1200-1360,* 1998.

McGinn, Bernard and Patricia Ferris McGinn. *Early Christian Mystics: The Divine Vision of Spiritual Masters,* 2003.

Meadow, Mary Jo. *Christian Insight Meditation: Following in the*

Footsteps of John of the Cross, 2007.

Meninger, William A. *The Loving Search for God: Contemplative Prayer and the Cloud of Unknowing,* 1998.

Merton, Thomas. *Contemplative Prayer,* 1971.

_____. *New Seeds of Contemplation,* 2007.

Nelstrop, Louise and Simon D. Podmore, *Christian Mysticism and Incarnational Theology: Between Transcendence and Immanence,* 2013.

Perez, Pablo. *Prayer Secrets: A Simple Blueprint to Help You Walk in the Presence of God,* 2014.

Peth, Howard. *The Dangers of Contemplative Prayer,* 2012.

Prophet, Elizabeth. *Becoming God: The Path of the Christian Mystic (Mystical Paths of the World's Religions),* 2010.

Rohr, Richard. *Falling Upward: A Spirituality for the Two Halves of Life,* 2011.

_____. *The Naked Now: Learning to See as the Mystics See,* 2009.

_____. *Immortal Diamond: The Search for Our True Self,* 2013.

_____. *Everything Belongs: The Gift of Contemplative Prayer,* 2003.

Schachter-Shalomi, Zaiman, Netanel Miles-Yepez, and Robert Michael Esformes. *Gate to the Heart: A Manual of Contemplative Jewish Practice,* 2013.

Suzuki, Daisetz Teitaro. *Christian and Buddhist,* 2011.

Thibodeaux, Mark E. *Armchair Mystic: Easing into Contemplative Prayer,* 2001.

Underhill, Evelyn. *Practical Mysticism: A Little Book for Normal People,* 2006.

_____. *The Complete Christian Mystic: A Practical, Step-By-Step Guide for Awakening to the Presence of God,* 2010.

_____. *Mysticism,* 2012.

_____. *The Cloud of Unknowing: A Guide to Contemplative Spirituality and Christian Mysticism,* 2014.

Vaughan-Lee, Llewellyn. *Prayer of the Heart in Christian and Sufi Mysticism,* 2012.

Vincent, Kristen E. *A Bead and a Prayer: A Beginner's Guide to Protestant Prayer Beads,* 2013.

Waller, Dennis Michael. *The Art of Talking to Christ: The Theory and Practices of Christian Mysticism,* 2011.

Walker, William. *Mystic Christianity or, The Inner Teachings of the Master,* 2012.

Zangano, Phyllis. *Mysticism and the Spiritual Quest: A Cross-cultural Anthology,* 2013.

GENERAL

Booth, Newell S. Jr. *African Religions: A Symposium,* 1977.

Eliade, Mircea. *From Primitives to Zen: A Thematic Sourcebook of the History of Religions.* New York: Harper & Row, 1967.

Lewis, Ioan M. "The Social Roots and Meaning of Trance and Possession," In *The Oxford Handbook of The Sociology of Religion,* edited by Peter B. Clark, 375-388. Oxford: Oxford University Press, 2009.

_____. *Ecstatic Religion,* 2nd ed. London: Routledge, 1989.

Martin, Walter, Jill Martin Rische, and Kurt Van Gorden. *Kingdom of the Occult.* Thomas Nelson, 2008.

Michaelsen, Johanna. *The Beautiful Side of Evil.* Harvest House, 1982.

Northcote, Jeremy. *The Paranormal and the Politics of Truth: A Sociological Account.* Charlottesville, VA: Imprint Academic, 2007.

Rouchet, G. *Music and Trance,* rev. English ed. Chicago: University of Chicago Press, 1985.

Thumma, Scott and Edward R. Gray, eds. *Gay Religion.* Lanham, MD: AltaMira Press, 2005.

Turner, Harold W. *Religious Innovation in Africa: Collected Essays on New Religious Movements,* 1979.

Wavell, Stewart, Audrey Butt, and Nina Epton. *Trances.* New York: E. P. Dutton & Co., 1967.

York, Michael. *Theology: Paganism as a World Religion.* New York: NYU Press, 2003.

INDEX

Note: Entries marked with * are also in the Glossary.

OTHER BOOKS BY KENT PHILPOTT

IF THE DEVIL WROTE A BIBLE

MEMOIRS OF A JESUS FREAK

AWAKENINGS IN AMERICA AND
THE JESUS PEOPLE MOVEMENT

HOW CHRISTIANS CAST OUT DEMONS TODAY

ARE YOU REALLY BORN AGAIN?
UNDERSTANDING TRUE AND FALSE CONVERSION

ARE YOU BEING DUPED?

WHY I AM A CHRISTIAN

FOR PASTORS OF SMALL CHURCHES

HOW TO CARE FOR YOUR PASTOR

Available at www.evpbooks.com

EVP

www.ingramcontent.com/pod-product-compliance
Lightning Source LLC
Chambersburg PA
CBHW051954090426
42741CB00008B/1382